READING JANE AUSTEN

Whether you're new to Austen's work or know it backward and forward already, this book provides a clear, full and highly engaging account of how Austen's fiction works and why it matters. Exploring new pathways into the study of Jane Austen's writing, novelist and academic Jenny Davidson looks at Austen's work through a writer's lens, addressing formal questions about narration, novel writing, and fictional composition as well as themes including social and women's history, morals and manners. Introducing new readers to the breadth and depth of Jane Austen's writing, and offering new insights to those more familiar with Austen's work, Jenny Davidson celebrates the art and skill of one of the most popular and influential writers in the history of English literature.

JENNY DAVIDSON is Professor of English and comparative literature at Columbia University, New York. Professor Davidson's previously published works include *Hypocrisy and the Politics of Politeness: Manners and Morals from Locke to Austen* (Cambridge, 2004), *Breeding: A Partial History of the Eighteenth Century* (2009) and *Reading Style: A Life in Sentences* (2014). She is the author of four novels, *Heredity* (2003), *The Explosionist* (2008), *Invisible Things* (2010) and *The Magic Circle* (2013).

READING JANE AUSTEN

JENNY DAVIDSON

Columbia University

CAMBRIDGE
UNIVERSITY PRESS

CAMBRIDGE
UNIVERSITY PRESS

University Printing House, Cambridge CB2 8BS, United Kingdom

One Liberty Plaza, 20th Floor, New York, NY 10006, USA

477 Williamstown Road, Port Melbourne, VIC 3207, Australia

314-321, 3rd Floor, Plot 3, Splendor Forum, Jasola District Centre, New Delhi - 110025, India

79 Anson Road, #06-04/06, Singapore 079906

Cambridge University Press is part of the University of Cambridge.

It furthers the University's mission by disseminating knowledge in the pursuit of education, learning and research at the highest international levels of excellence.

www.cambridge.org
Information on this title: www.cambridge.org/9781108431835
DOI: 10.1017/9781108367974

© Jenny Davidson 2017

First published 2017

A catalogue record for this publication is available from the British Library

ISBN 978-1-108-42134-8 Hardback
ISBN 978-1-108-43183-5 Paperback

For my mother, with love and friendship

Contents

Preface

I first read a battered yard-sale copy of *Pride and Prejudice* at the age of eight or nine. I am slightly ashamed to say that over the thirty-five years since then, I have probably read the novel as many as fifty times, although in recent years I am less likely to turn to it out of love or the need for comfort than because I am writing about it, and I still remember the thrill of teaching *Pride and Prejudice* as a PhD student and being given a "desk copy" of the Penguin edition: reading the book in a fresh edition felt almost like reading it for the first time. I love most of the authors I write about regularly – these include Swift, Richardson, Burke and Gibbon – but I don't turn to any of them especially for comfort or consolation. I love Austen in a different way than I love Swift or Burke, which invites the question of whether or not love and associated states like identification and immersion are at odds with the goals and values of criticism, which include objectivity and analytic traction.

The topic of how we respond to books we love, as well as how that affects the critical discourse about them, has become a legitimate object of study in its own right, with Austen as a central example; though Shakespeare might be the most closely comparable instance in the English literary tradition, certain other authors undoubtedly continue to elicit curiously strong allegiances from unusually large numbers of readers (the three quite different names of J. R. R. Tolkien, Ayn Rand and Toni Morrison come immediately to mind).[1] I strongly believe that rather than canceling each other out, a productive tension exists between the different modes involved in loving books and in reading them to understand how they work, what they mean and why they matter, not least because both orientations depend heavily on the practice of repeated rereading, even or perhaps especially in the case of books we already know very well.

I have said that I love Austen. I would go so far as to say that my knowledge of her novels colors almost every aspect of my relationships with people, books and the world at large. I also hold a degree of suspicion toward those who love Austen, though, myself included. Her work is by far the most popular subject I teach; an Austen seminar capped at eighteen might elicit seventy-five applications, and it will be tempting to dismiss out of hand all those submissions that blazon the student's love for Austen as the chief rationale for admission. Unfair as it may be, I have found that the student who rather dislikes Austen's fiction but wants to understand more about why others deem it interesting and important is more likely to contribute valuably to class discussion than the devoted admirer. One of the strongest tendencies that characterizes the admirer rather than the critic (of course I partake myself in both of these roles) involves talking about characters in novels as if they were real people, and while this may be another interesting and legitimate topic of recent literary-critical inquiry, as an unthinking habit, it tends to hamper conversation in a room where I mostly want to be talking about novelistic technique, social and political arguments and so forth.[2]

Austen's work isn't esoteric or difficult. The novels are relatively easy to understand at the level of language and plot. You don't really need to learn, as a reader of Austen, how to decode or decipher cryptic passages, and in this respect a book about reading Austen will have to take a somewhat different approach than one introducing readers to the work of a more obviously difficult writer like Milton or Joyce. Given that Austen's writing is already fairly accessible, then, what I want this book to do is to render it alluring to those who have not yet immersed themselves in her fictional worlds – and to make it strange to those who already know one or more of the novels well.

I also hope to counter the widespread but misleading notion that all of Austen's novels conform more or less perfectly to a fairy-tale romance plot. This premise, questionable even in the case of *Pride and Prejudice*, falls pretty quickly to pieces once you look at the other novels. As a corollary, I'd say that though any general book on Austen needs to give the reader significant new insights into *Pride and Prejudice* above all, insofar as it's her most popular novel both in and out of classrooms, one of the best ways to achieve that involves turning to the writings of Austen's earlier years. Both *Northanger Abbey* and *Sense and Sensibility* are especially valuable in this respect, as they show Austen experimenting with techniques of voice and narration that will be more subtly rendered in the later novels, sometimes so much so that their workings become virtually undetectable. Even apart from that, close attention to style and details of language will often open up new insights into the most familiar passages. Consider the sentences that describe Elizabeth Bennet's first sight of Mr. Darcy's estate:

> Elizabeth was delighted. She had never seen a place for which nature had
> done more, or where natural beauty had been so little counteracted by an
> awkward taste. They were all of them warm in their admiration; and at that
> moment she felt, that to be mistress of Pemberley might be something!
> (*PP* III.i, 271)

If you are resistant to the sheer pragmatism of the world of *Pride and Prejudice*, you may look askance at the information that the sight of his magnificent property makes Elizabeth Bennet feel differently about marrying Darcy. Is the novel celebrating material covetousness when it singles out this surge of feeling for special mention? A good answer to that question will have to delve deeply into both ethical and stylistic questions. In terms of substance, it's important to note that this is far from being the direct analog of a modern character rating one of her suitors more highly when she realizes that he drives a Maserati. The estate of Pemberley represents a set of values that are profoundly custodial, ethically synonymous with a compelling vision of a stable, successfully paternalistic society that is already in danger of being lost and whose preservation in Darcy's estate represents an almost fantastically appealing vision of a social order that is well-governed and benevolent rather than precarious and chaotic.

This is true, as far as it goes, but I think that the choice of words reveals something else, something equally important, about the narrator's orientation toward Elizabeth's sensation. Look again at those three sentences. Do they celebrate Elizabeth's moment of strong feeling (it might be pride, regret, desire or some other mixture of emotions), or does the construction of the sentence somewhat undercut Elizabeth's readiness to revise her opinion of Darcy based on the sight of his property? Is the tone "straight" or tongue in cheek, and if there's some slight ironic undermining here, at whose expense does it come? Would it reflect on Elizabeth's sudden swerve toward more conventional values than she has hitherto embraced, or even perhaps on the values of a society that has allowed property to become synonymous with ethical substance?

Style or diction will be one of the most important factors in making this kind of a determination. Narrative tone can be evaluated at specific moments, of course, but it is also developed continuously over a novel as a whole. When Elizabeth does come, slightly later on, to understand how well suited she and Darcy would have been as partners, the insight brings significant emotional pain, given that her sister's scandalous elopement with Wickham has pretty much ruled out the possibility of an alliance between the two families. At precisely this juncture, something strikingly ironic enters the narrative voice: "But no such happy marriage could now teach the admiring multitude what connubial felicity really was. An union of a different tendency, and precluding the possibility of the other, was soon to be formed in their family" (*PP* III.8, 344). Where does that sarcasm come from? Is it Elizabeth Bennet's own savagely self-protective irony, the scathing words (words that expose her own foolishness in fantasizing about a possibility now lost to her) offering compensation preemptively, in the face of a devastating foreclosure of possibility? Or does the irony derive principally from the narrator, and does it come at Elizabeth's expense and from outside her consciousness?

This kind of question can't have only one right answer. It will always be a matter of opinion. But becoming a more experienced and powerful literary critic involves honing your ability to marshal different kinds of evidence toward a coherent interpretation that might sway even a resistant reader toward your point of view. Thinking about style throughout Austen's novels (especially "free indirect style" and the mysterious verbal alchemy that lets a third-person narrator swoop freely in and out of different characters' consciousness) will let an individual reader amass a persuasive collection of evidence to support an argument about what's happening at moments like these; that kind of argument in turn provides traction on larger, more obviously significant questions about what values the novel endorses, which kinds of argument about society and human interaction it blocks and which it furthers.

There are a number of different possible routes through this book. Reading the chapters from start to finish provides an obvious default, and you won't go wrong proceeding in that fashion. Any given chapter can be read in isolation, though, if you have already homed in on a topic of interest and want to explore it in greater depth. If you are especially interested in formal questions about narration and novel-writing, you might turn first to the chapters on revision and voice, with the chapter on letters serving as a useful sequel. If you are interested in social history and women's history, the final chapter on female economies (an earlier working title was "Love and Loss") will be a good place to start. If you want to write novels yourself, the chapter on conversation probably offers the most immediate insights into fictional composition. If you are drawn to Austen's fiction because it presents a powerful set of arguments about ethics and human behavior, arguments that belong in conversation with contemporary arguments in the disciplines of sociology and moral philosophy, the chapters on manners and morals are a more obvious point of entry.[3] Equally, if you are reading only one of Austen's novels and don't want to have the others "spoiled" for you, you can use the index to navigate a path through this book that will prioritize readings and discussions of that particular book.

There must already be dozens of book-length treatments of Austen that proceed by considering each one of the major novels in chronological order, many of them very good, and I have recommended a few of my favorites in the suggestions for further reading that come at the end of this volume. References to Austen's works are given parenthetically in the text by volume, chapter and page number (I have used the Cambridge edition throughout), and I also refer occasionally to especially significant contemporary works and critical discussions whose details are provided in notes. Though chronology doesn't serve as this book's overriding rationale, I regularly consider questions of development over time, even as I move freely and associatively through the body of work Austen produced in a life that ended at the relatively early age of forty-one. Austen's work received only modest acclaim in her own time, but her reputation picked up momentum over the decades that followed, and for many years now she has been one of the single most popular and influential writers in the history of English literature.[4] This book shows why that should be so.

Acknowledgments

It is difficult to write appropriate acknowledgments for a book that is really the culmination of so many years of reading, writing and teaching. My views of Austen are strongly colored by my experience reading her novels with incredible teachers in college and graduate school, especially D. A. Miller, Claude Rawson and David Bromwich. Claudia L. Johnson was not my teacher in any formal sense, but her example continues to inspire me. When Linda Bree invited me to write this volume for the series, I seized the opportunity with huge excitement: she knows more about Austen than anybody else I know, but that is far from being the only reason that she is the ideal editor (indeed, the ideal reader) for this book. Her thoughtful comments on the manuscript have improved this book throughout. Thanks for the anonymous readers' reports on the proposal I submitted to the Cambridge University Press, and also for feedback from students and colleagues on a version of that proposal that Sarah Cole invited me to present in the Columbia Department of English and Comparative Literature's faculty works in progress series.

The undergraduates I've read Austen with are too many to name here, but I will thank them anyway for what I've learned reading Austen's novels in many different classrooms over several decades. Many graduate students, too, have helped me think more clearly about Austen and narration, but I must particularly thank two of my current doctoral students, Michael Paulson and Candace Cunard. My debt to Katie Gemmill for her work on conversation and the eighteenth-century novel is even more substantial; I have learned a great deal from her research and look forward to the book that will ensue. I regularly serve on committees for oral exams and dissertation defenses with departmental colleagues whose perceptiveness and learning about Austen as well as many other things gives me great pleasure: Nicholas Dames especially, but also Sharon Marcus, James Eli Adams, Erik Gray, Dustin Stewart and Julie Stone Peters. Teaching *Pride and Prejudice* in the context of Columbia's Literature Humanities sequence gave me a new perspective on why it is hard to teach Austen well, and I have benefited from conversation with course preceptors about their own experiences teaching the book. Others whose conversation about Austen and associated pleasures has helped me understand her writing better include Janet Min Lee, Tara Menon, Devoney Looser, Deborah Martinsen and Nicole Horesji.

I had an immersive initial spell of rereading in the peaceful environs of the Grandview Condominiums, Grand Cayman, courtesy of Brent Buckner, whose ability to welcome rather than merely tolerate my own frequent preference for reading over conversation is only one of the traits that make him my ideal partner. Life is also lightened and leavened by my brothers and their families, especially GG and Jack Maverick; my feline companions, Mickey and José; and my beloved grandfather Eugene Kilik, whose friendship has been one of the great pleasures of my life in New York. I belong to two communities (one online, one real-world) whose support and companionship make a huge difference to my daily quality of life: thanks to David Roche and the SWAP team, for keeping me reasonably consistent and reliably joyful as a runner; and to Joshua Hidalgo and the Chelsea Piers Powerlifting Team, for their strength, kindness and good humor.

I drafted most of this book during a truly idyllic term as Oliver Smithies Visiting Lecturer at Balliol College. Adam Smyth was an exemplary academic host, and the Oxford eighteenth-century community more generally provided warm welcome and support, Ros Ballaster especially. Victoria Holt's assistance in the college office was invaluable. A high point during that visit was the opportunity to present some thoughts about this project at one of Bruce's Brunches, courtesy of a lovely invitation from the Reverend Bruce Kinsey and the two student organizers of the series, Alexander Fuller and Eliza McHugh. My Mansfield Road (not Park) neighbor, Mary Fuller, was kind as well as sociable. Others whose conversation helped make the time in Oxford such a pleasure include David Russell, Kate McLoughlin, Jim McLaverty, Roger Lonsdale, Sir Drummond and Vivian Bone. Heartfelt thanks go to the teachers at YogaVenue, especially Susanne Kaesbauer; to Sy Wiggall; to the Oxford University Powerlifting Club; and to the gentleman with a bottle and newspapers who invariably greeted me, as I ran very slowly past his chosen bench in Christ Church Meadow, with encouraging words ("Good effort, miss!").

I finished most of the final revisions to the manuscript while enjoying the luxurious hospitality of the American Academy in Rome, courtesy of the Michael I. Sovern/Columbia University Affiliated Fellowship awarded by the Columbia University Provost's Office. Additional funds toward that stay were contributed by the office of the Dean of Humanities at Columbia, Sharon Marcus, and I am extremely grateful for Columbia's financial support as well as for the lively community I found at the Academy. I wrote this book during a full year of paid leave from my home institution, a fact that speaks to a remarkable degree of privilege in a time when the conditions for writing and publishing academic criticism have become difficult or impossible for many, and I would like to register at once my gratitude for that good fortune and my painful awareness of how rare it has come to be.

Reading Jane Austen is dedicated to my mother because anything else would be just plain wrong! She and I have been reading Austen together for more years than I can count. Her love and support are beyond measure; this book represents only an inadequate token of gratitude.

Abbreviations

All citations of Austen's writings are to the Cambridge Edition of the Works of Jane Austen, whose general editor is Janet Todd. Individual volumes are given as follows:

J	*Juvenilia*, ed. Peter Sabor (Cambridge: Cambridge University Press, 2006)
NA	*Northanger Abbey*, ed. Barbara Benedict and Deirdre Le Faye (Cambridge: Cambridge University Press, 2006)
SS	*Sense and Sensibility*, ed. Edward Copeland (Cambridge: Cambridge University Press, 2006)
PP	*Pride and Prejudice*, ed. Pat Rogers (Cambridge: Cambridge University Press, 2006)
MP	*Mansfield Park*, ed. John Wiltshire (Cambridge: Cambridge University Press, 2005)
E	*Emma*, ed. Richard Cronin and Dorothy McMillan (Cambridge: Cambridge University Press, 2005)
P	*Persuasion*, ed. Janet Todd and Antje Blank (Cambridge: Cambridge University Press, 2006)
LM	*Later Manuscripts*, ed. Janet Todd and Linda Bree (Cambridge: Cambridge University Press, 2008)
JAL	*Jane Austen's Letters*, 4th edn., ed. Deirdre Le Faye (2011; Oxford: Oxford University Press, 2014)
MJA	*A Memoir of Jane Austen and Other Family Recollections*, J. E. Austen-Leigh, ed. Kathryn Sutherland (Oxford: Oxford University Press, 2002)
FR	*Jane Austen: A Family Record*, 2nd edn., Deirdre Le Faye (1989; Cambridge: Cambridge University Press, 2004)

CHAPTER I

Letters

It's hard to imagine, immersed as we are in a boundless sea of multimedia messaging (texts, emails, calls on mobile phones and landlines, regular postal delivery and various overnight delivery services, newspapers, their digital analogues and other online news sites, broadcast television, seasons of television on DVD or Blu-Ray or streamed via the Internet, paper books and digital books that we read on handheld devices, social media from Twitter to Snapchat), the profound importance, the all-purpose utility, the sheer omnipresence for Austen and her contemporaries of the ordinary letter. Both in Austen's fiction and in her life, you get the sense that letters were often nearly everything, not least because a woman of modest means was unlikely to have independent control over her movements. Muddy roads, in the absence of a horse or carriage, could easily stop a genteel but income-constrained lady from walking even a few miles down the road to see a friend or relative, and unmarried adult women were often dispersed to relatives' establishments to live, separated from their closest female companions for long spells and sometimes even for whole lifetimes: letters offered the only way of staying close to loved ones outside the house.

In *Emma*, the impoverished Jane Fairfax, destined to earn her living as a governess, insists on walking to the post office even in the rain to see if there are any letters waiting for her. Emma's prosperous brother-in-law, John Knightley, tells the young woman that when she has lived to his age, she "will begin to think letters are never worth going through the rain for" (*E* II.16, 316), but Jane points out that once she is working as a governess, it is impossible that she will be "situated [as he is], in the midst of every dearest connection" (*E* II.16, 317). She does not expect, in other words, "that simply growing older should make me indifferent about letters": "You have every body dearest to you always at hand, I, probably, never shall again," she concludes forcefully; "and therefore till I have outlived all my affections, a post-office, I think, must always have power to draw me out, in worse weather than to-day" (*E* II.16, 317).

The letters of Austen's own that survive, out of a much larger number written in the novelist's lifetime, are not especially emotionally forthcoming. That may have less to do with Austen's temperament and relationships than with the ideas about privacy and decorum that governed her sister Cassandra's choice of which letters to keep and which to destroy after the writer's death. There are about a hundred and sixty of Austen's letters in the standard edition of her correspondence. Austen's niece Caroline speculated that Jane's letters to Cassandra (the two sisters were regularly separated in adulthood, most often when one or the other sister went for an extended stay in a married brother's household) "were, I dare say, open and confidential—My Aunt looked them over and burnt the greater part, (as she told me), 2 or 3 years before her own death—She left, or *gave* some as legacies to the Nieces—but of those that *I* have seen, several had portions cut out" (*MJA* 174).

The tone of the letters we do have is gossipy, affectionate, satirical and rarely deep, reflecting often on the practice of letter-writing itself. In one early letter to Cassandra, Austen observes: "I have now attained the true art of letter-writing, which we are always told, is to express on paper exactly what one would say to the same person by word of mouth; I have been talking to you almost as fast as I could the whole of this letter" (*JAL* 71). This language conveys both a joke about a silly piece of conventional wisdom (the true art of letter-writing surely extends further than mimicking face-to-face speech) and a deeper insight about the fact that writing a letter to someone one cares about can produce a feeling of closeness or intimacy. There is a good deal of comic throat-clearing around the question of how to write a decently long letter when you have nothing much to report, and questions of equity and reciprocity in letter-length also loom large: to her dear friend Martha Lloyd, in response to a "long Letter," which she claims was "valued as it ought" (*JAL* 216), Austen writes a lengthy response that concludes, "Now I think I may in Quantity have deserved your Letter. My ideas of Justice in Epistolary Matters are you know very strict" (*JAL* 217).

Roads were extended and improved throughout the eighteenth century in England, and river navigation acts and new canals improved the efficiency of water transport; stagecoaches made it easier not just for people but also for their letters and packages to be transported between different parts of the country, and as the British empire expanded overseas, so did incentives to find ways of allowing family members and business associates separated by great distances to correspond without untoward delays.[1] But though postal service became much faster, it wouldn't become cheap in

Britain until the introduction of a national penny post in 1840. In Austen's time, postage was still expensive enough that if you could get someone to carry your letter to its destination as a favor, you would very likely do so. The cost of postage, which was paid by the recipient rather than the sender, could also be avoided by using a so-called frank, allowed to members of Parliament for free postage; though it was illegal to share these, they were widely distributed to friends and relatives.

Allusions to the material details of transmission often form part of letters both real and fictional: "I had sent off my Letter yesterday before Yours came, which I was sorry for," writes Austen; "but as Eliza has been so good as to get me a frank, your questions shall be answered without much further expense to you" (*JAL* 193). This sort of context will help the reader of the novels decode allusions that otherwise might pass without notice. In *Persuasion*, when Anne Elliot's sister, writing from the country, says she can make her letter as long as she likes because a neighbor has offered to carry anything she wishes to Anne in Bath (*P* II.6, 178), she is referring to the fact that since the letter isn't traveling by official channels, Anne won't have to pay extra postage, which was then charged per sheet rather than by weight. There is a good deal of joking around this sort of question in Austen's own letters: "It is throwing a Letter away to send it by a visitor, there is never convenient time for reading it–& Visitor can tell most things as well.—I <u>had</u> thought with delight of saving you the postage—but Money is Dirt" (*JAL* 256). Money was not really dirt: both Austen and her characters preferred to save the postage when they could.

Austen wrote with a quill pen whose nib she would periodically have dipped into an inkwell to fill; she used iron gall ink, which could easily be transported as a powder and mixed when needed.[2] Her niece Caroline later recalled that "every note and letter of hers, was finished off *handsomely*— There was an art *then* in folding and sealing—no adhesive envelopes made all easy—some people's letters looked always loose and untidy—but *her* paper was sure to take the right folds, and *her* sealing wax to drop in the proper place—" (*MJA* 171). Writing in those days was sometimes accommodated by way of furniture tailor-made for the purpose: there is a record of Austen's father purchasing in December 1794, probably for his daughter's nineteenth birthday and at a cost of twelve shillings, "a small Mahogany Writing Desk with 1 Long Drawer and Glass Ink Stand Compleat," which seems to be the desk that survives as a family heirloom and is now owned by the British Library (*FR* 89).

Modern editors of eighteenth-century letters will often give information about the physical nature of manuscripts as they encountered them in libraries and archives. Not all letters are transcribed from originals in the author's own hand; they might be copies made by friends or relations or heavily edited versions, published in an earlier era, of original texts that are now lost. The technical nomenclature (seal, wafer, watermark) may be evocative, but it doesn't necessarily convey the glorious materiality of eighteenth-century letters as their original readers would have experienced them. The size, texture and overall quality of the paper would have told a recipient a good deal about what kind of a letter she was getting, as would the handwriting and the closeness with which the sheet was written. Adopting mourning dress for close family members didn't just involve wearing black clothes, it had an analog for self-presentation in writing: "I have forgotten to take a proper-edged sheet of Paper," writes Austen in a letter composed just after her uncle's death, alluding to the practice of using paper with a black border in a mourning household (*JAL* 355).

Covering a sheet of paper with writing and then turning it upside down or sideways and writing between the lines ("crossing") was also common, not just because paper was expensive but due to the high cost of postage. In this sense, writing "closely" isn't just a question of manners or decorum (respecting one's correspondent and presenting oneself formally in writing), it actually helps keep down the recipient's postage costs. A long letter might be seen as a gesture of simultaneous generosity and aggression, or at the very least carelessness, just as a letter with relatively few words on the page might not seem to give good value for money: "Your close-written letter makes me quite ashamed of my wide lines," Austen writes (*JAL* 157). In *Emma*, the voluble Miss Bates says of her niece Jane's letter – the letter that Emma resists having to hear read aloud – that she "really must, in justice to Jane, apologise for her writing so short a letter—only two pages you see—hardly two—and in general she fills the whole paper and crosses half" (*E* II.1, 168). Her elderly mother, Miss Bates adds, calls it "chequer-work," a little joke that conveys something of the heart and soul that are poured into these meticulously textured missives.

Jane Fairfax's letters are regularly shared with as many other members of the village as will stop to listen to them, and the communal nature, in this period, of a letter's audience – it is rarely written exclusively for the attention of the person whose name features as addressee – is very striking. *Pride and Prejudice* gives another instance of how much the sharing of letters would have been thought of as a default mode rather than an anomaly. Lydia's letters home from Brighton "were always long expected, and always very short" – these are the letters written to her mother and then shared with the rest of the family – "and from her correspondence with her sister," the narrator adds, "there was still less to be learnt—for her letters to Kitty, though rather longer, were much too full of lines under the words to be made public" (*PP* II.19, 264). This may not refer to underlining for emphasis, although Austen herself does sometimes underline for that reason in her own letters, but rather to a simple code in which the letter-writer would underline certain letters and words to pick out a "secret" message, one safeguard for privacy in a world where letters were usually shared among family members once they had been read by their initial addressee.

Both gender and social class can be thought of as having pronounced effects on the style of a letter and the forms it might take, though the generalizations Austen's characters make about how people write letters are usually more humorous than apt. In *Northanger Abbey*, when Henry Tilney claims (it is a form of flirtation) "that the usual style of letter-writing among women is faultless, except in three particulars" (*NA* I.3, 20), Catherine falls for the conversational lure. She asks what those particulars are, and is told by Henry: "A general deficiency of subject, a total inattention to stops, and a very frequent ignorance of grammar." Women are supposed to write longer and fuller but also more trivial letters than men because their male counterparts are living busier lives in the world and accordingly have less time and inclination to write copiously, but when Mary Crawford asserts, in *Mansfield Park*, that brothers' letters are overly laconic, the often reticent Fanny Price registers a strong dissent: when brothers are "at a distance from all their family," she insists, "they can write long letters" (*MP* I.6, 70). Fanny's own brother William is a midshipman serving overseas in the Navy, so that the two siblings' correspondence has served for many years as their sole means of retaining intimacy, just as it did for Austen herself and the two brothers of hers who went into the navy. In *Emma*, farmer Robert Martin proposes marriage to Harriet Smith by letter; Emma doesn't want Harriet to marry Robert Martin (she is sure Harriet can do better), but she is taken aback when Harriet shows her the letter. It is such a very good letter – manly, open, honest, plainspoken – that she disingenuously suggests to Harriet that his sisters must have helped him write it (*E* I.7, 53).

We need not think about Austen's time as being at great historical distance from our own in order to understand the ways that a letter may sometimes have greater communicative power than speech. Many of us find that we are able to be more honest, to reveal vulnerabilities and share our most private concerns, more easily in writing than in face-to-face conversation, with a safety net coming into being when physical presence is taken altogether out of the question. The conclusion of *Persuasion* provides a lovely instance of writing allowing a person to speak more directly and openly even than speech itself. Captain Wentworth proposes to Anne Elliot by way of a letter written desperately, passionately while in her immediate physical presence and during a conversation she is having with another man about differences in how men and women experience love and the passage of time. (I will have more to say about this scene in Chapter 3, "Revision.")

Of course, we also sometimes inappropriately fall back on writing rather than speech because we are afraid of how the other person will respond to what we wish to convey, and Austen is extremely sensitive to the nuances of such tensions. Edmund Bertram, quite unsure as to whether or not Mary Crawford will accept his proposal of marriage, writes in a letter to Fanny Price that in preference either to visiting Mary in London where she is now staying (her frivolous surroundings there don't favor serious Edmund's solemn suit) or to waiting to propose in person when she comes back to the country in the summer,

> I believe I shall write to her. I have nearly determined on explaining myself by letter. To be at an early certainty is a material object. My present state is miserably irksome. Considering every thing, I think a letter will be decidedly the best method of explanation. I shall be able to write much that I could not say, and shall be giving her time for reflection before she resolves on her answer, and I am less afraid of the result of reflection than of an immediate hasty impulse; I think I am. (*MP* III.13, 490)

But Austen has been sly in creating this letter. We discern strong elements of indecision and even of rationalization in Edmund's words; each assertion, even as it is expressed, exposes itself as wishful thinking and opens up a keen awareness for the reader of the possibility that the opposite is true. When Edmund says, after another swathe of agonizing oscillation back and forth, "I think I shall certainly write" (*MP* III.13, 491), we can hear the oxymoron in the wording (the uncertainty of "think" unsuccessfully countered by the false sureness of "certainty") even more strongly than we did in that opening ("nearly determined").

Here is another, more elaborate scene in which Austen explores the relationship between convention and feeling in letter-writing. Look at the progression that takes place in this passage from *Mansfield Park*:

> Every body at all addicted to letter writing, without having much to say, which will include a large proportion of the female world at least, must feel with Lady Bertram, that she was out of luck in having such a capital piece of

> Mansfield news, as the certainty of the Grants going to Bath, occur at a time when she could make no advantage of it, and will admit that it must have been very mortifying to her to see it fall to the share of her thankless son, and treated as concisely as possible at the end of a long letter, instead of having it to spread over the largest part of a page of her own.—For though Lady Bertram rather shone in the epistolary line, having early in her marriage, from the want of other employment, and the circumstance of Sir Thomas's being in Parliament, got into the way of making and keeping correspondents, and formed for herself a very creditable, common-place, amplifying style, so that a very little matter was enough for her; she could not do entirely without any; she must have something to write about, even to her niece, and being so soon to lose all the benefit of Dr. Grant's gouty symptoms and Mrs. Grant's morning calls, it was very hard upon her to be deprived of one of the last epistolary uses she could put them to. (*MP* III.13, 493)

The term "common-place" here doesn't mean ordinary; it refers to the rhetorical technique of "commonplacing" – offering a moral platitude or apothegm of some kind that is then "amplified" or developed in a formulaic manner. This is why "a very little matter was enough for her": writing in this mode is less about transmitting information or feelings than about rehearsing platitudes and recapitulating various forms of conventional wisdom, pious or otherwise. Austen's irony here is affectionate rather than ruthless, I would say, with the humor coming gently rather than savagely at Lady Bertram's expense.

The irony turns darker, though, in the sentences that follow. "There was a rich amends, however, preparing for her," the narrator comments, with Lady Bertram's "hour of good luck" coming when there is "some very alarming intelligence" to "communicate" (*MP* III.13, 493). The oldest Bertram son, Tom, has fallen very ill at his friends' house, but even such a high-quality piece of news goes through the sausage-making machine of Lady Bertram's amplifying style, and Austen has fun producing a long passage of pastiche or parody of a style that is superficial, formal, virtually without feeling. "Fanny's feelings on the occasion were indeed considerably more warm and genuine than her aunt's style of writing," the narrator continues (*MP* III.13, 495), but in the meantime Lady Bertram continues to pass on her other son's accounts of Tom's illness to Fanny

> in the same diffuse style, and the same medley of trusts, hopes, and fears, all following and producing each other at hap-hazard. It was a sort of playing at being frightened. The sufferings which Lady Bertram did not see, had little power over her fancy; and she wrote very comfortably about agitation and anxiety, and poor invalids, till Tom was actually conveyed to Mansfield, and her own eyes had beheld his altered appearance. Then, a letter which she had

been previously preparing for Fanny, was finished in a different style, in the
language of real feeling and alarm; then, she wrote as she might have spoken.
"He is just come, my dear Fanny, and is taken up stairs; and I am so shocked
to see him, that I do not know what to do. I am sure he has been very ill.
Poor Tom, I am quite grieved for him, and very much frightened, and so is
Sir Thomas; and how glad I should be, if you were here to comfort me."
(*MP* III.13, 495)

It takes the sharp shock of Tom's actual appearance to let real feeling break
through the shell of Lady Bertram's manner.

Letters may also reveal things that their authors don't intend. A good
example of this can be found in Mr. Collins' letters in *Pride and Prejudice*,
where Austen allows the letter-writer to condemn himself in his own words
for comic effect. Mr. Bennet's heartless amusement at Mr. Collins' expense
models the reader's own distaste: "There is a mixture of servility and self-
importance in his letter," he comments to Elizabeth, "which promises
well" (*PP* I.13, 71). Another correspondent seen to reveal her true self in
her letters is Lucy Steele in *Sense and Sensibility*. Lucy's letters also let
Austen show us the potential for a letter that purports to be written to one
person to be really designed to reach a different reader's eyes. News has
broken of Lucy's secret longtime engagement to Edward Ferrars, with
whom Elinor Dashwood is in love, and Lucy writes a distinctly passive-
aggressive letter to Elinor in which she exults over her in the guise of
thanking her for standing by Lucy in the wake of the unpopular revelation.
Lucy is also angling, though, for assistance (financial or otherwise) from
Elinor's host, Mrs. Jennings, and when Elinor finishes reading the letter,
"she performed what she concluded to be its writer's real design, by placing
it in the hands of Mrs. Jennings, who read it aloud with many comments of
satisfaction or praise" (*SS* III.2, 315).

This scene also demonstrates the ways in which individual readers'
responses to a given letter tell us a great deal about them. Mrs. Jennings'
noncritical and approving comments on Lucy's manipulative letter reveal
a significant disparity of taste and judgment between Elinor and herself,
with Elinor's own greater awareness of the letter's falseness and hidden
agendas strongly framing the letter for the reader. The shameless or brazen
quality of Lucy's letter-writing voice may come through most clearly in the
brief and explicit letter she sends Edward at the end of the novel, after she
has married his brother instead. It is full of sentimental clichés ("I scorn to
accept a hand while the heart was another's") and relies on a slangy short-
hand ("Sincerely wish you happy in your choice") that is in marked
contrast to the finer decorum of the Dashwood sisters' epistolary manner

(*SS* III.13, 413). Edward comments wryly to Elinor that "this is the only letter I ever received from her, of which the substance made me any amends for the defect of the style" (*SS* III.13, 414).

Another example of the ways that letter-writing can be used instrumentally to draw out and develop observations about character comes in a well-known scene near the opening of *Pride and Prejudice*. Elizabeth Bennet is staying at Netherfield Park while her sister is ill, and she and the other members of the party spend the evening together in the drawing room pursuing their own separate activities. Mr. Darcy is writing a letter to his sister, and Miss Bingley, who wishes he would pay more attention to her, is "watching the progress of his letter, and repeatedly calling off his attention by messages to his sister" (*PP* I.10, 51). Elizabeth watches their interactions with amusement (the third-person narrative voice here is strongly colored by Elizabeth's perspective and point of view): "The perpetual commendations of the lady either on his hand-writing, or on the evenness of his lines, or on the length of his letter, with the perfect unconcern with which her praises were received, formed a curious dialogue, and was exactly in unison with her opinion of each" (*PP* I.10, 51).

Now that they are talking about letters, their host, Mr. Bingley, makes this assertion about his own style of writing. His sister has claimed that he "writes in the most careless way imaginable. He leaves out half his words, and blots the rest" (*PP* I.10, 52), but he puts a different spin on the matter: "My ideas flow so rapidly that I have not time to express them," he says, "—by which means my letters sometimes convey no ideas at all to my correspondents" (*PP* I.10, 52). Elizabeth claims to find Bingley's humility disarming, but Darcy offers a counter-suggestion that the appearance of humility can often conceal an indirect boast: "you are really proud of your defects in writing," he tells his friend, "because you consider them as proceeding from a rapidity of thought and carelessness of execution, which if not estimable, you think at least highly interesting" (*PP* I.10, 53). He goes on to suggest that Bingley overrates the "power of doing any thing with quickness," citing as evidence his friend's own comment that if he ever decides to leave Netherfield he will be gone in five minutes, which Darcy says is not the "sort of panegyric, of compliment" that Bingley intends. Darcy adds, moreover, that he is not convinced Bingley would leave so quickly if a friend asked him to stay, and the yielding quality (based on trust and affection) that they all discern in Bingley will become an important plot point when we learn of Bingley's abrupt departure from Netherfield and, later on, of the part Darcy played in convincing his friend to go. All this characterization of the differences between the two friends, up to and including the foreshadowing of events to come, is occasioned by the initial scene of letter-writing.

Letters are not just crude instruments of character; there are other ways in which they transmit meanings to a perceptive reader that may not have been fully legible even to the letter-writer him- or herself. A series of letters can become an especially powerful lens for understanding a person's feelings as they may have changed over time. When Elizabeth revisits the question of what effect disappointment in the wake of Bingley's abrupt departure has had on her sister, she rereads the letters Jane has written her over the past months:

> They contained no actual complaint, nor was there any revival of past occurrences, or any communication of present suffering. But in all, and in almost every line of each, there was a want of that cheerfulness which had been used to characterize her style, and which, proceeding from the serenity of a mind at ease with itself, and kindly disposed towards every one, had been scarcely ever clouded. Elizabeth noticed every sentence conveying the idea of uneasiness, with an attention which it had hardly received on the first perusal. (*PP* II.ii, 210)

This is an example of how what is not said in a letter may be as significant as the words that do appear on the page.

Here is another example that shows how it may be a formal or superficial aspect of the letter, not its substance as such, that serves as the primary agent of meaning. *Emma*'s Mr. Woodhouse is unable to keep to the point, and the modern reader might easily dismiss his comment in this instance as an irrelevancy, but when Mr. Woodhouse says of Frank Churchill's letter to his father and stepmother that "it was an exceeding good, pretty letter, and gave Mr. and Mrs. Weston a great deal of pleasure. I remember it was written from Weymouth, and dated Sept. 28th—and began, 'My dear Madam,' but I forget how it went on; and it was signed 'F.C. Weston Churchill.'—I remember that perfectly" (*E* I.ii, 103), he is not merely rambling. His daughter Isabella, though she is not a creature of intellectual sharpness, responds, "How very pleasing and proper of him!" – which is to say that the gesture of signing himself with his birth father's name as well as the name of his wealthier adoptive family itself may be the most signal piece of intelligence transmitted, a meaningful gesture of goodwill.

Another important way in which letters transmit meaning concerns not only what they say and don't say but the very fact of correspondence, which in certain circumstances itself becomes an important piece of information. This is partly a question of manners – decorum strongly held in this period that unmarried young women of a certain social class should not correspond with men outside the family unless and until they were actually promised to each other in marriage, with the approval of both sets of parents – but it also has a distinguished literary history. Richardson's influential and immensely popular epistolary novel *Clarissa, or The History of a Young Lady* (1748) is concerned among other things to suggest that Clarissa's initial agreement to correspond with Lovelace contains the seed of her ultimate downfall. Lovelace has insinuated himself into the position of correspondent because Clarissa's uncle has asked Lovelace to write a series of letters to serve as a relative's guide for the Grand Tour, the trip that young men of means would take during this period to see the society and art of the continent. Clarissa tells her friend and chief correspondent, Anna Howe, that Lovelace "consented, on condition that I would *direct* his subjects, as he called it" (this passage also has the advantage of showing the ways in which a correspondence might have the same kind of entertainment value that we would now associate with a book, a magazine or a television series):

> and as everyone had heard his manner of writing commended, and thought his relations might be agreeable amusements in winter evenings; and that he could have no opportunity particularly to address me in them, since they were to be read in full assembly before they were to be given to the young gentleman, I made the less scruple to write, and to make observations and put questions for our further information—Still the less, perhaps, as I love writing; and those who do are fond, you know, of occasions to use the pen: and then, having everyone's consent, and my uncle Hervey's desire that I would, I thought that if I had been the only scrupulous person, it would have shown a particularity that a vain man would construe to his advantage, and which my sister would not fail to animadvert upon.[3]

Clarissa's explanations sound a little strained – they have the air of rationalization – and Anna remonstrates in response that by the sheer fact of corresponding with him at all, Clarissa has rendered herself vulnerable:

> Already, in order to restrain him from resenting the indignities he has received and which are daily offered him, he has prevailed upon you to correspond with him privately. I know he has nothing to boast of from *what* you have written. But is not his inducing you to receive his letters, and to answer them, a great point gained?—By your insisting that he should keep this correspondence private, it appears that there is *one secret* that you do not wish the world should know; and *he* is master of that secret. He is indeed *himself*, as I may say, that secret!—What an intimacy does this beget for the lover!—How is it distancing the parent! (L10, 71)

Anna's language powerfully conflates Lovelace, the correspondence and the secret into one dangerous knot of transgression.

Critic Tom Keymer has written especially well about the ways the letter in this period could be seen as completely transparent, completely manipulative or falling at any point on the spectrum between those two poles.[4] Epistolary fictions – novels written in the form of a series of letters – can be found earlier as well, but it was Richardson who consolidated the form of the epistolary novel at mid-century and proselytized successfully for its powers. His first novel, *Pamela, or Virtue Rewarded* (1740), was hugely popular, but it also provoked a backlash from readers who felt that the heroine was too good to be true, manipulative rather than honest, a schemer (Henry Fielding's parody, *Shamela* (1741), perfectly captures the key elements of the hostile take on Pamela's modes of writing about herself). It was neither *Pamela* nor *Clarissa* but Richardson's final novel, *Sir Charles Grandison* (1753), that was Austen's favorite (it was also favored by many other writers of the period, including historian Edward Gibbon). "Her knowledge of Richardson's works was such as no one is likely again to acquire," Austen's nephew wrote in his memoir of her: "Every circumstance narrated in Sir Charles Grandison, all that was ever said or done in the cedar parlour, was familiar to her; and the wedding days of Lady L. and Lady G. were as well remembered as if they had been living friends" (*MJA* 71).

Marianne Dashwood is the character of Austen's who most narrowly escapes something like Clarissa's tragic fate; another young woman in *Sense and Sensibility*, the ward of Colonel Brandon (we don't meet her directly), is indeed seduced and abandoned by Marianne's lover Willoughby, who reads like a sort of late-stage reimagining of Richardson's Lovelace. Although Marianne's rash entrance into a correspondence with the man she loves derives most immediately from her unwillingness to obey conventions she deems meaningless, the novel taken as a whole seems to confirm the argument that even a convention that appears outdated or unnecessary can sometimes be defended on the grounds of its power to limit our own emotional vulnerability. Marianne regularly accuses Elinor of being overly conventional or scrupulous, but the novel aligns pretty strongly with the older sister's point of view on this matter. It is emotionally risky for Marianne to send a letter to a man to whom she is not engaged, and Willoughby's failure to respond to her letters has the painful quality of what we might call in our own time "blanking" or "ghosting" (*SS* II.4, 188).

In this scene, Elinor and her sister Marianne have just arrived in town and are both writing letters. Elinor, not so much probing for information as thinking pragmatically about news to be reported and the economizing of writerly effort, suggests that since she herself is writing to their mother just now, Marianne might delay her own letter home:

> "I am *not* going to write to my mother," replied Marianne hastily, and as if wishing to avoid any farther inquiry. Elinor said no more; it immediately struck her that she must then be writing to Willoughby, and the conclusion which as instantly followed was, that however mysteriously they might wish to conduct the affair, they must be engaged. (*SS* II.4, 183)

To Elinor, in other words, more prudent than her sister, the mere fact of a correspondence between Marianne and Willoughby *must* mean that they have become engaged without telling anyone else. Shortly after this scene, when Colonel Brandon sees a letter in the servant's hand "directed to Mr. Willoughby in [Marianne's] writing," he too assumes that a correspondence signifies an engagement: "I came to inquire," he says to Elinor, "but I was convinced before I could ask the question. Is every thing finally settled? Is it impossible to—? But I have no right, and I could have no chance of succeeding" (*SS* II.5, 197).

Austen loved Richardson, but she was also stylistically indebted to Fielding, whose morals were considered less respectable than Richardson's but who was one of the eighteenth century's great comic writers, and it is chiefly in the mode of parody that we find the novel of letters affecting Austen's choices as a young writer. The set of stories we refer to as the juvenilia or early works survives in fair copies contained in three volumes, and gives a fascinating window into Austen's literary concerns in the years of her childhood and adolescence. A number of her short early fictions, including "Love and Freindship" and "Lesley Castle," are written in an epistolary format, a mode invoked during this stage of Austen's writing life less for melodrama or tragedy than for satire predominantly. *Lady Susan* represents a more extended and consistent epistolary fiction than either of those two others. It is slightly reminiscent of Laclos' novel *Dangerous Liaisons* (1782), although there is no evidence that Austen read that novel, whose deeply scandalous sexual subject matter would have made it difficult for a country parson's daughter to get her hands on it: though it is certainly a moralist's treatment of adulterous sex rather than a celebration of libertine morality, one of the novel's most memorable scenes involves the libertine Valmont writing that he has used the naked body of the woman he's in bed with "as a desk on which to write to my beautiful devotee."[5]

The title character of *Lady Susan* is a Machiavellian schemer whose self-serving machinations know no bounds. Only her sister-in-law seems to see through her, and the comedy of the letters often arises from the sharp juxtaposition of Lady Susan's account of her own actions with descriptions of those same actions provided by a hostile onlooker. Lady Susan herself speaks of her sister-in-law Mrs. Vernon as follows (this brief passage will show both the maddening narcissism and the real charm of Lady Susan's letter-writing style):

> I wanted her to be delighted at seeing me—I was as amiable as possible on the occasion—but all in vain—she does not like me.—To be sure, when we consider that I did take some pains to prevent my Brother-in-law's marrying her, this want of cordiality is not very surprising–& yet it shews an illiberal & vindictive spirit to resent a project which influenced me six years ago, & which never succeeded at last. (*LM* 13)

After an implausibly fast-paced series of flirtations and rapprochements – speeding things up is one way of producing a sharply satirical or comic effect, a key tactic for Fielding in *Shamela* – the sequence of letters breaks off at a point well short of what would have constituted a full-length novel. It is hard to know whether Austen had become impatient with the story or simply with the mode of narration: "This Correspondence," interrupts a hitherto unknown narrator, "by a meeting between some of the Parties & a separation between the others, could not, to the great detriment of the Post office Revenue, be continued longer" (*LM* 75).

Though all six of Austen's published novels are narrated in the third person, two of them were probably initially drafted in the epistolary mode, as novels written in letters. These are *Sense and Sensibility* and *Pride and Prejudice*, and the last part of this chapter will concentrate on a few moments when the underlying epistolary scaffolding seems to obtrude through each story as we now experience it. There are complex tradeoffs for a novelist choosing between these two modes of narration: the epistolary mode has immediacy on its side, allowing the reader an immersive identification with the novel's characters in the role of addressee especially (we read a letter just as it would have been read by its recipient), while third-person narration has much greater advantages in the way of perspective, contextualization and summing up, letting the writer claim the authority of an impartial historian rather than being implicated as a potentially biased player in the events at hand.

The culture, too, was moving away from the epistolary mode over Austen's own reading lifetime. James Raven observes that between 1750 and 1760 new novels in letters averaged roughly a tenth of each year's total new fiction, "but by 1766 and 1768 nearly one quarter annually and in 1769 more than one third of all new novel titles were epistolary": it would go on to be the case that at least thirty percent of novels published between 1770 and 1790 were in letters, and in certain years the proportion reached as high as two-thirds.[6] Raven says that the turning point seems to have come around 1791, and that by the final few years of the century, "the epistolary form had lost its popularity, swamped, it seems by the diversity and directness of new historical and Gothic narratives that were not well-suited to relation by imaginary letters."

Perhaps the clearest legacy of *Sense and Sensibility*'s previous life as a novel written mostly or entirely in letters can be seen in the extent to which the central dramatic encounter in the first half of the novel – Marianne Dashwood's rejection by Willoughby – comes chiefly by way of the reader gaining access to the letters the two have exchanged. Marianne has come from the country largely to facilitate her reunion with the man she loves, and she begins by sending him several short letters to let him know she is in town. Still not having heard back from him, she spots Willoughby at a party and makes herself known, but rather than responding warmly to her greeting, he acknowledges her only with distance and coldness (*SS* II.6, 200–01). The sequel to this scene of rebuff comes not long after, in the privacy of the sisters' bedroom at Mrs. Jennings' house. At breakfast, Elinor sees Marianne receive a letter and run from the room; when she follows and opens the door, she finds Marianne "stretched on the bed, almost choked by grief, one letter in her hand, and two or three others lying by her" (*SS* II.7, 207). It would hardly be an exaggeration to say that in Austen's world we experience our most intense sorrows in privacy and via the medium of the letter.

Marianne now passes the sheaf of letters to Elinor and we read them with her. First there is Willoughby's cold rejection, whose language strikes Elinor as almost unbelievable:

> Though aware, before she began it, that it must bring a confession of his inconstancy, and confirm their separation for ever, she was not aware that such language could be suffered to announce it! Nor could she have supposed Willoughby capable of departing so far from the appearance of every honourable and delicate feeling—so far from the common decorum of a gentleman, as to send a letter so impudently cruel: a letter which, instead of bringing with his desire of a release any professions of regret, acknowledged no breach of faith, denied all peculiar affection whatever—a letter of which every line was an insult, and which proclaimed its writer to be deep in hardened villainy. (*SS* II.7, 209)

Then, with Elinor, we read the sequence of earlier letters that fills in the backstory, Marianne's brief affectionate notes letting Willoughby know she is in town: the first is confident, the second disappointed, the third devastated following the encounter at the party (*SS* II.7, 212–13). But Elinor's sympathy for her sister – her ability to feel her sister's pain – doesn't prevent her from having reservations about the correspondence having come about in the first place:

> That such letters, so full of affection and confidence, could have been so answered, Elinor, for Willoughby's sake, would have been unwilling to believe. But her condemnation of him did not blind her to the impropriety of their having been written at all; and she was silently grieving over the imprudence which had hazarded such unsolicited proofs of tenderness, not warranted by anything preceding, and most severely condemned by the event[.] (*SS* II.7, 214)

The most pressing underlying rationale for punctilio or decorum may depend on emotional self-protection: Elinor is desperate for Marianne to become more prudent not primarily because self-exposure attracts the negative attention of others, though that is also a legitimate concern, but because having others witness our emotional pain only exacerbates and deepens it.

In *Pride and Prejudice*, the scene in which Darcy proposes to Elizabeth Bennet, though it possesses its own dramatic intensity, is characterized by miscommunication rather than perfect understanding. It is the letter Elizabeth receives from Darcy in the chapter following that has the far more profound effect on her intellect and emotions, and it is felt by many readers that Elizabeth's reading of the letter – and the feelings and thoughts she experiences in its aftermath – constitutes the novel's emotional fulcrum. Darcy hands the letter to Elizabeth in person after finding her on her walk in the park at Rosings; it is "an envelope containing two sheets of letter paper, written quite through, in a very close hand.—The envelope itself was likewise full" (*PP* II.12, 218). This is an unexpectedly long letter, in other words, and it is also a document that will plunge Elizabeth into confusion and uncertainty: "Her feelings as she read were scarcely to be defined," says the narrator (*PP* II.13, 226). That phrase "scarcely to be defined" may sound to modern ears merely noncommittal, but it would have had the connotation for contemporary readers of something genuinely too intense and bewildering to be put into language.

What the letter asserts about the history of Bingley's relationship with Jane Bennet seems unforgivable to Elizabeth – "It was all pride and indolence," notes the narrator, in a nice instance of the stylistic device called free indirect style, which is to say that we are hearing Elizabeth's own thought as it has migrated into an unmarked third-person voice – but she is able to read the account of Wickham's history with clearer attention. Her initial response is to put the letter aside, "protesting that she would not regard it, that she would never look in it again" (*PP* II.13, 227), but "in half a minute the letter was unfolded again, and collecting herself as well as she could, she again began the mortifying perusal of all that related to Wickham, and commanded herself so far as to examine the meaning of every sentence" (*PP* II.13, 227). After reading and rereading the particulars of the transactions, Elizabeth faces a conundrum:

> She put down the letter, weighed every circumstance with what she meant to be impartiality—deliberated on the probability of each statement—but with little success. On both sides it was only assertion. Again she read on. But every line proved more clearly that the affair, which she had believed it impossible that any contrivance could so represent, as to render Mr. Darcy's conduct in it less than infamous, was capable of a turn which must make him entirely blameless throughout the whole. (*PP* II.13, 227–28)

The letter can be seen in this as in many other instances to be susceptible of kinds of honesty and truthfulness that social interactions are more likely to conceal than expose.

It is largely Wickham's personal charm of manner that has allowed him to make such a very good impression on Elizabeth, though when she reconsiders her conversations with him she is "*now* struck with the impropriety of such communications to a stranger, and wondered it had escaped her before" (*PP* II.13, 229). Similarly, when Elizabeth revisits what Darcy has said about Jane, especially his expressed conviction that Jane wasn't in love with Bingley (an opinion supported by an independent observation made by Charlotte Lucas about Jane's calmness of manner and its potential for misconstrual), her ideas are turned upside down:

> She grew absolutely ashamed of herself.—Of neither Darcy nor Wickham could she think, without feeling that she had been blind, partial, prejudiced, absurd.
> "How despicably have I acted!" she cried.—"I, who have prided myself on my discernment!—I, who have valued myself on my abilities! . . . Had I been in love, I could not have been more wretchedly blind. But vanity, not love, has been my folly.—Pleased with the preference of one, and offended by the neglect of the other, on the very beginning of our acquaintance, I have courted prepossession and ignorance, and driven reason away, where either were concerned. Till this moment, I never knew myself." (*PP* II.13, 230)

Letters in *Pride and Prejudice* facilitate not just emotional change but also more traditional forms of plot development. As the novel moves into its final phase, Elizabeth receives two letters from her sister, one of which has been missent elsewhere because the address (the "direction," to use Austen's nomenclature) had been written "remarkably ill" (*PP* III.4, 301). This is itself already a signal to Elizabeth that something must be wrong at home, and indeed what begins as an ordinary letter (we are not given the actual text) is supplemented by a second half, "dated a day later, and written in evident agitation" (*PP* III.4, 301), which tells Elizabeth that their sister Lydia has eloped with Wickham. Elizabeth feels personally responsible for this development, and when Darcy finds her shortly afterward, she tells him everything: "When I consider ... that *I* might have prevented it!—*I* who knew what he was. Had I but explained some part of it only—some part of what I learnt, to my own family! Had his character been known, this could not have happened. But it is all, all too late now" (*PP* III.4, 305–06). Thus the arrival of the letter, and the immediate distress into which it casts Elizabeth, provides the occasion for Elizabeth to confess to Darcy that she has come to believe what he wrote in his earlier letter, and to confide that her orientation to him now differs markedly from before. Elizabeth does not reveal all her feelings to Darcy at this juncture, but she admits them to herself with a striking degree of honesty (the third-person narrator has full access to her thoughts and emotions): "never had she so honestly felt that she could have loved him, as now, when all love must be vain" (*PP* III.4, 306), observes the narrator, a feeling that prompts Elizabeth to throw "a retrospective glance over the whole of their acquaintance, so full of contradictions and varieties, sigh[ing] at the perverseness of those feelings which would now have promoted its continuance, and would formerly have rejoiced in its termination" (*PP* III.4, 307).

The denouements of the last volume continue to depend on letters, which offer a high degree of economy for storytelling: there is Lydia's thoughtless letter in the wake of her elopement, and everything it reveals about her character and attitudes (*PP* III.5, 321), Mr. Bennet's failure to keep everyone up to date on news ("His family knew him to be on all common occasions, a most negligent and dilatory correspondent, but at such a time, they had hoped for exertion" (*PP* III.6, 324)), the odious letter from Mr. Collins ("The death of your daughter would have been a blessing in comparison of this" (*PP* III.6, 327)), Mr. Gardiner's more level-headed and exhaustive account of the current situation, the exchange of letters between Elizabeth and her aunt when Lydia (now home) drops a hint accidentally of Mr. Darcy's presence at the wedding – and finally a comic sequence of letters in conclusion.

The first, given in full, is from Elizabeth to her aunt; the second, its text omitted, from Mr. Darcy to his aunt; and the last (and shortest one quoted) is from Mr. Bennet to Mr. Collins. It recounts the news of Elizabeth's engagement to Darcy and concludes, "Console Lady Catherine as well as you can. But, if I were you, I would stand by the nephew. He has more to give" (*PP* III.18, 424). The letter, then, in this last stretch of the novel seems to have become a sort of universal tool for the novelist, a powerful and highly economical instrument for storytelling whose integration into third-person narration, sometimes in direct quotation but also often in summary or paraphrase, represents an essential component of Austen's fictional technique.

CHAPTER 2

Conversation

The opening line of the first chapter of *Pride and Prejudice* is probably the most famous sentence Austen ever wrote. "It is a truth universally acknowledged, that a single man in possession of a good fortune, must be in want of a wife" (*PP* I.1, 3) – with the ring of a maxim or apothegm, the words capture some of the feel of eighteenth-century rights discourse (we may be reminded of the well-known early sentence in the Declaration of Independence that runs, "We hold these truths to be self-evident, that all men are created equal, that they are endowed by their Creator with certain unalienable Rights, that among these are Life, Liberty and the pursuit of Happiness"), only with a demented and self-interested twist. Most men of good fortune are *not* in need of wives, and any need in the case can more rationally be apportioned to the young women of little means who seek husbands to mend their fortunes.

Even more formally striking and strange than this opening sally is the fact that the rest of the first chapter is made up almost exclusively of direct speech, a remarkably ruthless and efficient technique for plunging us into the novel's world. Austen shows us rather than merely telling us about the playful perversity of Mr. Bennet, the querulous demanding irrationality of Mrs. Bennet and the asymmetry of the relationship between husband and wife. The chapter is remarkably sparing of third-person narration in the usual form of description, speech tags (the "he saids" and "she saids" that authors use to organize their accounts of speech) and so forth. Austen wrote in a letter, after she had received copies of the first edition of *Pride and Prejudice*, that "There are a few Typical errors—& a 'said he' or a 'said she' would sometimes make the Dialogue more immediately clear—but 'I do not write for such dull Elves'" (*JAL* 210). By "Typical" Austen must mean "typographical," which is to say printer's errors, but it is more relevant that she acknowledges the book's extremely parsimonious use of speech tags. Defoe's narrators (Moll Flanders is a good example) use such speech tags copiously, and as speakers of English and oral storytellers we have a strong cognitive preference for such marking or tagging gestures. As Austen allows, minimizing speech tags will occasionally risk loss of clarity as to who's speaking, but the tradeoffs are evident: it is more stylistically striking and far more economical, foregrounding the speech of characters themselves and allowing their own words to show us who they are, how they think and what matters about them in relation to the other people in their lives. The allusion at the end of the comment is to Scott's poem *Marmion*, whose lines run: "I do not rhyme to that dull elf / Who cannot image to himself" (*JAL* 420 n. 5), and Austen's invocation of the poem shows the extent to which she wants her reader to enter a relationship of textual reciprocity in which the author is not the only one who works to create meaning.

The word "conversation" had a more extended range for eighteenth-century writers than it has for us now, not least because of the centrality of conversation to the salon culture of Enlightenment France. It meant not only talking with someone but also consorting or otherwise having dealings with them, perhaps with a considerable degree of intimacy: the word sometimes served as a thinly veiled euphemism for sexual intercourse, and "criminal conversation" (abbreviated "*crim. Con.*") was the name for the suit a husband could bring for damages against a man who had sex with his wife. Earlier in the eighteenth century, Swift had parodied the banalities of fashionable talk in *Polite Conversation* (it was a compilation of foolish pronouncements, the work of several decades, completed around 1731 and published in 1738), but many earnest manuals were published during this period to teach people to converse properly, just as other manuals sought to instruct readers in polite letter-writing.

Few of Austen's most memorable speakers would serve as exemplars of polite conversation, and the sense of conversation as an art in her novels (great conversation has something in common with chamber music) is often outweighed by the abuse of the power of speech by some of its possessors. Biographer Claire Tomalin identifies a series of "obsessed and eloquent women" in Austen's writing, singling out the letter-writer Charlotte in the early unpublished work titled "Lesley Castle" as an early member of the sequence (loquacity can be expressed on paper as well as in a spoken monologue) and naming Mrs. Bennet, Mrs. Norris of *Mansfield Park* and Miss Bates of *Emma* as three of her chief successors.[1] Speech for all of these women serves less as a means of communication or a tool of sociability (gossip in human communities is supposed to be closely related to physical grooming among groups of monkeys) than as the running expression of an interior monologue that is antithetical to real communication. Miss Bates, always saying too much and too little at the same time, has been deemed by many modern readers a creation of genius, but Austen's choices in *Emma* puzzled contemporary readers. Novelist Maria Edgeworth, having liked *Mansfield Park* and *Pride and Prejudice* very much, is on the record as having found *Emma* perplexing: "There was no story in it, except that Miss Emma found that the man whom she designed for Harriet's lover was an admirer of her own – & he was affronted at being refused by Emma & Harriet wore the willow – and smooth, thin water gruel is according to Emma's father's opinion a very good thing & it is very difficult to make a cook understand what you mean by smooth thin water gruel!!" (quoted in *FR* 231).

Miss Bates outdoes even Mr. Woodhouse when it comes to the flow of trivialities. When news comes to the little circle in Highbury that Mr. Elton is engaged to be married to a Miss Hawkins (the name conveys a certain lack of social distinction as well as something of the predatory nature of the hawk), the conversation that ensues is at once intolerably rambling and thoroughly mortifying to Emma, still pained by the memory of Mr. Elton's proposal of marriage to herself rather than to her friend Harriet, the bride she intended for him. Here is one of Miss Bates' contributions to the exchange:

> A Miss Hawkins.—Well, I had always rather fancied it would be some young lady hereabouts; not that I ever—Mrs. Cole once whispered to me—but I immediately said, 'No, Mr. Elton is a most worthy young man—but'—In short, I do not think I am particularly quick at those sort of discoveries. I do not pretend to it. What is before me, I see. At the same time, nobody could wonder if Mr. Elton should have aspired.—Miss Woodhouse lets me chatter on, so good-humouredly. She knows I would not offend for the world. (*E* II.3, 189)

Miss Bates doesn't *mean* to suggest that Emma led Mr. Elton on, and her sheer volubility discourages close attention, not just on the part of her initial auditors but from the readers of the novel as well. Her words provide hard evidence, though, that Mr. Elton's aspirations have been the subject of gossip in the community. The speech reveals Miss Bates to be tactless, naïve, hypersensitive to the feelings of others and yet incapable of censoring herself in advance when she is about to touch on a topic that is inappropriate or uncomfortable.

Speech in Austen's novels is often hugely self-revealing, inexorably drawing out self-involved and self-interested aspects of the speaker's character. Miss Bates and Mr. Woodhouse mostly elicit the reader's pity, and in

Emma it is the character of Mrs. Elton whose speech reveals the most culpable forms of self-interest and bias. The words Austen uses to mark Mrs. Elton's fluctuations of mood on the day of the visit to Donwell Abbey are especially remarkable in this regard:

> The whole party were assembled, excepting Frank Churchill, who was expected every moment from Richmond; and Mrs. Elton, in all her apparatus of happiness, her large bonnet and her basket, was very ready to lead the way in gathering, accepting, or talking—strawberries, and only strawberries, could now be thought or spoken of.—"The best fruit in England—every body's favourite—always wholesome.—These the finest beds and finest sorts.—Delightful to gather for one's self—the only way of really enjoying them.—Morning decidedly the best time—never tired—every sort good—hautboy infinitely superior—no comparison—the others hardly eatable—hautboys very scarce—Chili preferred—white wood finest flavor of all—price of strawberries in London—abundance about Bristol—Maple Grove—cultivation—beds when to be renewed—gardeners thinking exactly different—no general rule—gardeners never to be put out of their way—delicious fruit—only too rich to be eaten much of—inferior to cherries—currants more refreshing—only objection to gathering strawberries the stooping—glaring sun—tired to death—could bear it no longer—must go and sit in the shade." (*E* III.6, 389–90)

"Such, for half an hour, was the conversation," the narrator adds, the word "conversation" in this instance carrying some weight of irony given that what has been provided is a monologue, not an exchange with the kinds of mutuality the term "conversation" would normally imply. We hear Mrs. Elton's initially triumphant mood – and her slightly preposterous or at least mildly nonsensical assertions about picking strawberries oneself being "the only way of really enjoying them" – give way to what we can think of as her default mode, boasting about her prosperous relatives in Bristol and revealing her tendency to battle for dominance with social underlings. She is popping berries into her mouth while she picks, we imagine, and by the end of this flow of conversation she has thoroughly sickened herself both of strawberries and of being outside in the sun.

This passage also demonstrates something notable about Austen's use of inverted commas as quotation marks. They are much more flexible tools at this stage than they would later become (Austen is really at the cusp of standardization of punctuation in printed fiction – we suspect, though we don't know, that this punctuation would have been added by the printer to a manuscript whose scenes of dialogue may have been less clearly marked).[2] In our own time, if I use quotation marks, it means the words inside correspond exactly to what the person said, but Austen uses them in conjunction not only with direct speech but also with the third-person reporting of speech. In this particular case, Mrs. Elton's speech is reported in a sped-up third-person summary that heightens the satirical effect.

Elsewhere quotation marks can sometimes signal thought, speech merely internal rather than words uttered aloud. This is a nice example from *Northanger Abbey*, whose protagonist, Catherine, is increasingly suspicious of her host, General Tilney, the father of her friends Henry and Eleanor: "An hour passed away before the General came in, spent, on the part of his young guest, in no very favourable consideration of his character.—'This lengthened absence, these solitary rambles, did not speak a mind at ease, or a conscience void of reproach'" (*NA* II.8, 187). Catherine can't be speaking these words out loud – she hasn't confided her suspicions to her friends. The words are uttered only to herself and in her own mind, and the verb she chooses has passed, in the process of translation to the third person, from the present tense of thought (a conjectural "do not speak") to the past tense. The migration of thought into narration is related to the formal technique called "free indirect style" or "free indirect speech," which will be treated more fully in Chapter 6, "Voice."

One of Austen's most striking gifts as a novelist derives from her ear for the peculiarities of individual speech, and in particular for the configurations of words we use when we want to rationalize selfishness or otherwise cover up, possibly even to ourselves and certainly to others, the less attractive motives that really drive our choices and actions. As is often the case, we can spot simpler versions of this technique in Austen's own real-life correspondence. In a letter to her sister, Cassandra, Austen writes of the wife of their brother James (the brother who had moved with his family into the parsonage at Steventon, displacing sisters and parents from their longtime home) that "Mrs. J.A. does not talk much of poverty now, though she has no hope of my brother's being able to buy another horse *next* summer" (*JAL* 121). In capturing her sister-in-law's small verbal affectation and transferring it to third-person summary, Austen delicately exposes the gap between a self-serving profession of one's own limited means, delivered preemptively to those who might otherwise expect some overflow of bounty, and external evidence of one's prosperity.

The lack of generosity some well-off people display in the face of their less prosperous relatives, as well as the excuses and protestations they utter in situations where they might be expected to extend some kind of financial assistance, is a great target of satire in Austen's fiction as well. A nice instance can be seen in *Sanditon*, the novel Austen left incomplete when she died. Our protagonist, Charlotte, is talking to the penny-pinching Lady Denham, who has inherited a good deal of money from one husband and a title from another. It is Lady Denham's boast that when her second husband died, she made his nephew a gift of his gold watch:

> She said this with a look at her companion which implied its right to produce a great impression—and seeing no rapturous astonishment in Charlotte's countenance, added quickly—
>
> "He did not bequeath it to his nephew, my dear—it was no bequest. It was not in the will. He only told me, and *that* but once, that he should wish his nephew to have his watch; but it need not have been binding, if I had not chose it.—" (*LM* 178)

The narrator's point of view here is clearly aligned with Charlotte's (the irony of "no rapturous astonishment" may even derive from Charlotte's own clear-eyed view of this bit of selfishness), and we can hear the comic self-serving elaboration in the words that come next from Lady Denham's mouth, accentuated by the minor grammatical solecism of "chose" for "chosen," which reminds us that despite her title, she is not herself of the most refined and genteel quality.

A supreme example of the ways in which conversation reveals processes of rationalization around self-interested behavior comes in *Sense and Sensibility*'s Mrs. John Dashwood. It is one of the great comic turns in all of Austen's fiction. Her own covetous nature prompts her to persuade her husband, over the course of a couple of chapters, that there is no need to be generous to his disinherited sisters, and the initial extended conversation between husband and wife is the most prominent feature of the novel's opening. John Dashwood, half-brother of the three Dashwood girls by their father's first marriage, has promised their father on his deathbed "to do every thing in his power to make [the girls] comfortable" (*SS* I.1, 5). He will go on insensibly to talk himself out of his initial commitment, and the narrative checks in with him at intervals, each time noting the difference the passage of time has made to his intentions and convictions:

> When he gave his promise to his father, he meditated within himself to increase the fortunes of his sisters by the present of a thousand pounds a-piece. He then really thought himself equal to it. The prospect of four thousand a-year, in addition to his present income, besides the remaining half of his own mother's fortune, warmed his heart and made him feel capable of generosity.—"Yes, he would give them three thousand pounds: it would be liberal and handsome! It would be enough to make them completely easy. Three thousand pounds! He could spare so considerable a sum

with little inconvenience."—He thought of it all day long, and for many days successively, and he did not repent. (*SS* I.1, 6)

You see the by now familiar use of the quotation marks for what are probably thoughts rather than spoken words, given in the third person so that it reads more like summary or paraphrase than direct speech.

In the following chapter, Austen produces a bravura instance of persuasion that begins with a third-person restatement of Mrs. John Dashwood's position (she has already stated her objections to the initial proposal):

> Mrs. John Dashwood did not at all approve of what her husband intended to do for his sisters. To take three thousand pounds from the fortune of their dear little boy, would be impoverishing him to the most dreadful degree. She begged him to think again on the subject. How could he answer it to himself to rob his child, and his only child too, of so large a sum? And what possible claim could the Miss Dashwoods, who were related to him only by half blood, which she considered as no relationship at all, have on his generosity to so large an amount. It was very well known that no affection was ever supposed to exist between the children of any man by different marriages; and why was he to ruin himself, and their poor little Harry, by giving away all his money to his half sisters? (*SS* I.2, 9–10)

This is not yet free indirect style – there is too clear a relationship between the person talking and the third-person reporting of the words – but we might think of it as a transitional third-person mode that points the way to Austen's later development of the powerful and versatile tool of free indirect speech.

The narration then segues into directly reported conversation. "Well, then," says Mrs. Dashwood at one point early on,

> "*let* something be done for them; but *that* something need not be three thousand pounds. Consider," she added, "that when the money is once parted with, it never can return. Your sisters will marry, and it will be gone for ever. If, indeed, it could ever be restored to our poor little boy—"
>
> "Why, to be sure," said her husband, very gravely, "that would make a great difference. The time may come when Harry will regret that so large a sum was parted with. If he should have a numerous family, for instance, it would be a very convenient addition." (*SS* I.2, 10–11)

The adverb "gravely" is sly here; the narrator shows her own position on the matter. (I use the gendered pronoun as a provocation rather than because I really think we can say definitely that one of Austen's disembodied narrators has such a thing as a gender, although it's worth noting that the title page of the first published novel informs the reader simply that it is

"By a Lady," and there may be some common presumption of shared gender identity between author and narrator when not otherwise specified.) This notation of manner, though it might seem a simple matter of description, submits John Dashwood to the reader's unfavorable judgment, and by the end of the conversation, his wife has talked him first into reducing the amount of the proposed gift to each sister from a thousand pounds to a mere five hundred, then to funding an annuity for their mother instead – but then "people always live for ever when there is any annuity to be paid them; and she is very stout and healthy, and hardly forty. An annuity is a very serious business; it comes over and over every year, and there is no getting rid of it" (*SS* I.2, 12). She goes on to point out that an even better option would be simply an occasional present of fifty pounds or so, because (as John Dashwood persuades himself) "they would only enlarge their style of living if they felt sure of a larger income" (*SS* I.2, 13); finally, once Mrs. Dashwood puts into words her conviction that she is convinced that her husband's father "had no idea of your giving them any money at all," the amount of the gift is reduced to exactly nothing.

Speech and conversation offer the medium in which Austen best demonstrates the operation of mean-spirited and ungenerous motives on ourselves and others, and reporting conversation also allows her to show the effects of a strong-minded and selfish partner's persuasion on a weaker party. The technique continues to be mobilized throughout the novel, and another installment of the same ongoing process of rationalization can be found in a subsequent conversation between John Dashwood and Elinor (*SS* II.11, 255–57), an encounter that prompts this ironic comment from the narrator on the brother's mix of feelings: "He had just compunction enough for having done nothing for his sisters himself, to be exceedingly anxious that everybody else should do a great deal; and an offer from Colonel Brandon, or a legacy from Mrs. Jennings, was the easiest means of atoning for his own neglect" (*SS* II.11, 259).

A more subtle or sophisticated version of this technique can be seen in chapter 3 of *Persuasion*, one of my favorite scenes in all of Austen's fiction. The attorney Mr. Shepherd, determined to repair the finances of his oblivious client, here wants to manipulate his employer, Sir Walter Elliot, into accepting the idea that Admiral Croft and his wife – for now, he's not naming them, just hinting suggestively about naval officers – will be the best possible tenants for Kellynch Hall, Sir Walter having grudgingly accepted that he must rent it out. When the appearance-obsessed Sir Walter objects to the fact that admirals have such weather-beaten faces, Mr. Shepherd's daughter Mrs. Clay (a supreme manipulator and flatterer,

like a hyper-charged version of *Sense and Sensibility*'s Lucy Steele)
intervenes:

> "Nay, Sir Walter," cried Mrs. Clay, "this is being severe indeed. Have a little
> mercy on the poor men. We are not all born to be handsome. The sea is no
> beautifier, certainly; sailors do grow old betimes; I have often observed it;
> they soon lose the look of youth. But then, is not it the same with many
> other professions, perhaps most other? Soldiers, in active service, are not at
> all better off; and even in the quieter professions, there is a toil and a labour
> of the mind, if not of the body, which seldom leaves a man's looks to the
> natural effect of time. The lawyer plods, quite care-worn; the physician is up
> at all hours, and travelling in all weather; and even the clergyman—" she
> stopt a moment to consider what might do for the clergyman;—"and even
> the clergyman, you know, is obliged to go into infected rooms, and expose
> his health and looks to all the injury of a poisonous atmosphere." (*P* I.3,
> 22–23)

Conversation as a mode or medium does of course offer opportunities to
individual participants that go beyond persuasion and domination.
Another important kind of verbal exchange in Austen's fiction is the
conversation as attack on a secret or not-so-secret enemy, such interactions
falling along a spectrum from passive aggression to regular old-fashioned
straightforward aggression. Think of the moment in *Sense and Sensibility*
when Lucy Steele confides in Elinor about her longstanding secret engagement to Edward Ferrars, who has fallen in love with Elinor in the meantime
(she reciprocates his unspoken feelings). When Lucy suggestively mentions
the Ferrars family as her future in-laws, Elinor asks whether she's alluding,
as her possible spouse, to Edward's younger brother, Robert – "'No,'
replied Lucy, 'not to Mr. *Robert* Ferrars—I never saw him in my life;
but,' fixing her eyes upon Elinor, 'to his elder brother'" (*SS* I.22, 148).
The emphasis on the first name is knowing, needling, and the narrator
notes that significant detail concerning Lucy's gaze as another way of
underlining something about Lucy's motives, in case the words she utters
have not yet made them sufficiently clear. (Watch out in Austen for that use
of the tactical descriptive phrase, attached to quoted speech, to draw the
reader's attention to motive by way of manner.)

Austen powerfully sustains the reader's sense of Lucy's malice toward
Elinor over a succession of exchanges between the two women. In their
next conversation, when Lucy wonders out loud whether Elinor was
offended by her communication, Elinor politely demurs, in terms that
themselves play with the overlap between the sincere and the disingenuous: "Could you have a motive for the trust, that was not

honourable and flattering to me?" she asks Lucy (*SS* II.2, 167). The answer of course is yes, probably something like unseemly gloating at having vanquished a despised competitor, and Lucy declines to take Elinor's question at face value: "'And yet I do assure you,' replied Lucy, her little sharp eyes full of meaning, 'there seemed to me to be a coldness and displeasure in your manner, that made me quite uncomfortable'" (*SS* II.2, 167). Lucy's older sister is in on the secret, and when Mrs. Jennings later jokes about Elinor's "beau" Edward, saying that he is not a great coxcomb ("he is one of the modestest, prettiest behaved young men I ever saw; but as for Lucy, she is such a sly little creature, there is no finding out who *she* likes"), the elder Miss Steele can't let it go without another malicious comment – here, again, the narrator notes something about the physical delivery of the lines to bring home the unpleasantly knowing manner of the spoken intimation:

> "Oh!" cried Miss Steele, looking significantly round at them, "I dare say Lucy's beau is quite as modest and pretty behaved as Miss Dashwood's."
> Elinor blushed in spite of herself. Lucy bit her lip, and looked angrily at her sister. (*SS* II.2, 170)

And in a final act of verbal aggression, this one remote, Lucy sends a distinctly misleading message to Elinor via the Dashwood family servant to say that she now bears the name Mrs. Ferrars. Elinor naturally assumes that Lucy has married Edward at last, and when he appears in person at their house, she asks him, awkwardly, about "Mrs. Ferrars": she means to refer, appropriately, to Edward's new wife. When Edward assumes she's asking after his mother, Elinor corrects the misapprehension, emphasizing that she meant to inquire "after Mrs. *Edward* Ferrars":

> He coloured, seemed perplexed, looked doubtingly, and after some hesitation, said,
> "Perhaps you mean—my brother—you mean Mrs.—Mrs. *Robert* Ferrars."
> "Mrs. Robert Ferrars!"—was repeated by Marianne and her mother, in an accent of the utmost amazement;–and though Elinor could not speak, even *her* eyes were fixed on him with the same impatient wonder. He rose from his seat and walked to the window, apparently from not knowing what to do; took up a pair of scissars that lay there, and while spoiling both them and their sheath by cutting the latter to pieces as he spoke, said, in a hurried voice,
> "Perhaps you do not know—you may not have heard that my brother is lately married to—to the youngest—to Miss Lucy Steele." (*SS* III.12, 407–08)

The narrator's account of Edward's behavior here is loosely akin to those briefer notations about meaningful glances and sharp little eyes – it supplements and enlivens the words uttered in the conversation by speaking to an aspect of the character's state of mind as it is revealed in small physical movements. Edward's anxiety about the whole situation (and especially, we imagine, about the fact that he is now free not just to propose to Elinor but also to bear her reproaches for the pain his past choices have entailed for her) is brought to life very vividly by the visual observation of him unconsciously cutting apart the sheath with the scissors. Here the effect is to give emotional depth to his distress, whereas the previous examples seem more obviously designed to highlight mixed motives or feelings at odds with the words uttered.

Several examples in *Northanger Abbey* give an even clearer notion of the technique. Early in that novel, Isabella affects to have been rendered self-conscious and shy by the unwanted attentions of two young men, and she asks our protagonist, Catherine, to walk with her further away from them, repeatedly questioning Catherine as to whether the men are following and insisting that she will ignore them if they are. But when Catherine, "with unaffected pleasure, assured [Isabella] that she need not be longer uneasy, as the gentlemen had just left the Pump-room," Isabella's response gives away her underlying motive: "'And which way are they gone?' said Isabella, turning hastily round. 'One was a very good-looking young man'" (*NA* I.6, 36). The technique here is a little cruder and more obvious than what we see in *Sense and Sensibility*, but simpler examples help us understand the internal construction of some of the apparently seamless moments in the later fiction.

Elsewhere in *Northanger Abbey*, when Isabella makes an oblique allusion, comprehensible to the reader but opaque to the unsophisticated Catherine, to the fact that there is more than one way they might become sisters-in-law (i.e., not by Isabella marrying Catherine's brother, but by Isabella and Catherine both marrying Tilney brothers), the narrator notes parenthetically that her words are uttered "(with a blush)" (*NA* II.3, 148) – this locution is so economical that it doesn't even need a verb. Isabella and Lucy are both somewhat unattractive characters, culpably selfish in their motives, but there are ways of being self-involved that are just human rather than being particularly ethically culpable, and *Sense and Sensibility* also gives us many other examples of how speech – and the novelist's decisions about how to report it – reveals thought. Consider the funny and poignant scene in which Marianne Dashwood, increasingly troubled by Willoughby's failure to join her in London at his earliest opportunity, persuades herself that the current good weather may be keeping him in the country (he is an enthusiastic hunter). She talks out loud to herself, moving through a series of thoughts and associations, with the narrator again giving us that little extra prod in the form of a parenthetical notation of manner: in this case, "(with a little return of anxiety)" (*SS* II.5, 190). Marianne's thoughts are so transparent that Elinor intervenes with a distraction, "wishing to prevent Mrs. Jennings from seeing her sister's thoughts as clearly as she did" (*SS* II.5, 190).

Each scene of this sort carries its own mix of simple description and pointed judgment. Marianne's preoccupation with Willoughby is unfortunate but natural, the novel suggests (Elinor only wishes she would conceal it more thoroughly from others to spare herself from greater pain), but often characters in Austen's fiction who proceed through this kind of associative rationalization are thoroughly condemned by the evidence of their own words. I am thinking in particular of a passage in *Persuasion* that is not a spoken conversation but one of those internal debates that Austen brings to life so well. Anne's oldest sister, Elizabeth, demoted from her high-status residence at Kellynch Hall to a fashionable but small set of apartments in Bath, is now faced with a social conundrum:

> Elizabeth was, for a short time, suffering a good deal. She felt that Mrs. Musgrove and all her party ought to be asked to dine with them, but she could not bear to have the difference of style, the reduction of servants, which a dinner must betray, witnessed by those who had been always so inferior to the Elliots of Kellynch. It was a struggle between propriety and vanity; but vanity got the better, and then Elizabeth was happy again. These were her internal persuasions.—"Old fashioned notions—country hospitality—we do not profess to give dinners—few people in Bath do—Lady Alicia never does; did not even ask her own sister's family, though they were here a month: and I dare say it would be very inconvenient to Mrs. Musgrove—put her quite out of her way. I am sure she would rather not come—she cannot feel easy with us. I will ask them all for an evening; that will be much better—that will be a novelty and a treat. They have not seen two such drawing rooms before. They will be delighted to come to-morrow evening. It shall be a regular party—small, but most elegant." (*P* II.10, 238)

"Persuasion" is of course also the keyword-style title given to the novel as a whole, though not by Austen herself (family tradition suggests she thought of calling it *The Elliots* (*FR* 238)), and this comic and relatively trivial instance of "internal persuasions" is given depth and poignancy, in the larger context of the novel, by our awareness of what it has cost Anne to yield all those many years ago to the "persuasion" of Lady Russell.

The extent to which this technique of Austen's is most often used to expose cruelty and self-serving rationalization rather than other, more sympathetic forms of feeling becomes especially clear if we look at the character of Mrs. Norris in *Mansfield Park*. Mrs. John Dashwood has a negative material effect on the fortunes of the Dashwood sisters, but neither Elinor nor Marianne is particularly vulnerable to emotional wounding from her; Fanny Price is far more sensitive to the kinds of disparagement she experiences at the hands of her domineering aunt. The novel repeatedly dramatizes mean feelings (mean in both senses, given that Mrs. Norris is always miserly and often cruel); sometimes they are brought to life in third-person passages that follow Mrs. Norris' internal persuasions, to use that phrase again, but more often they appear in spoken conversations whose fidelity of reporting is so strongly allied with a form of judgment that it risks tipping over into satire.

In an early scene, when Fanny worries that the time may have come for her to be sent away from the big house to stay with Mrs. Norris in the village, her cousin Edward tries to allay her concerns by praising the advantages of her moving in with Mrs. Norris. Speech here has clearly migrated into the third-person narration: Edward's attempt to reassure Fanny, says the narrator, could have been spared,

> for Mrs. Norris had not the smallest intention of taking her. It had never occurred to her, on the present occasion, but as a thing to be carefully avoided. To prevent its being expected, she had fixed on the smallest habitation which could rank as genteel among the buildings of Mansfield parish; the White house being only just large enough to receive herself and her servants, and allow a spare room for a friend, of which she made a very particular point;–the spare-rooms at the parsonage had never been wanted, but the absolute necessity of a spare-room for a friend was now never forgotten. (*MP* I.3, 31–32)

We hear Mrs. Norris' speaking voice in that "only just large enough to receive herself and her servants, and allow a spare room for a friend" – then the narrator comes back in, and we move a little further away from the sound of the character's own speaking voice when it is noted that the spare rooms at the parsonage were never used. The repetition of "the absolute necessity of a spare-room for a friend" reveals the utterance to be self-serving cant by the simple means of quoting Mrs. Norris' own words.

Here is another relevant passage. This one uses quotation marks for that close third-person paraphrase of Mrs. Norris' highly distinctive speech. Fanny's brother William has received a commission as lieutenant in the Navy, a development that comes at the behest of Henry Crawford and with no expense or trouble to Sir Thomas Bertram:

> Mrs. Norris seemed as much delighted with the saving it would be to Sir Thomas, as with any part of it. "*Now* William would be able to keep himself, which would make a vast difference to his uncle, for it was unknown how much he had cost his uncle; and indeed it would make some difference in *her* presents too. She was very glad that she had given William what she did at parting, very glad indeed that it had been in her power, without material inconvenience just at that time, to give him something rather considerable; that is, for *her*, with *her* limited means, for now it would all be useful in helping to fit up his cabin. She knew he must be at some expense, that he would have many things to buy, though to be sure his father and mother would be able to put him in the way of getting every thing very cheap—but she was very glad that she had contributed her mite towards it."
>
> "I am glad you gave him something considerable," said Lady Bertram, with most unsuspicious calmness—"for *I* gave him only 10*l*."
>
> "Indeed!" cried Mrs. Norris, reddening. "Upon my word, he must have gone off with his pockets well lined! And at no expense for his journey to London either!" (*MP* II.13, 352–53)

Here are displayed a number of the traits with which this chapter has been concerned: the marking of Mrs. Norris' speech for emphasis (the italics here are used to pick out a sort of running refrain of self), the tactical notation of physical detail to emphasize something about delivery (Mrs. Norris reddening with anger or perhaps a hint of embarrassment). Family tradition had it, by the way, that the "rather considerable" sum given by Mrs. Norris to her nephew was one pound (*MJA* 119), and Austen regularly entertained her nieces and nephews with this sort of extratextual detail.

My attention here to the finer details of the way that third-person narration incorporates snippets of speech, moving effortlessly between the indirect reporting of speech and the full-on representation of actual conversation, may have led me to neglect some other significant uses of conversation in the novels. Many of the novels can be thought of as a series of conversations on a set of related topics, a structure that's especially striking in the case of *Mansfield Park*, where conversations and arguments about ordination, the ethics of amateur theatricals, the Englishness of Shakespeare and a host of other topics in some sense constitute the mechanism that moves the novel forward. In the closing section of this chapter, though, I will instead look at what may be the greatest moment of interplay between the conversation and the letter in all of Austen's fiction, a scene that can be thought of as the ultimate weaving together of the techniques laid out in my two initial chapters.

I am referring to the scene at the end of *Persuasion* where Captain Wentworth eavesdrops on Anne's conversation with Captain Harville at the same time as he is writing a letter to Anne that turns out itself to be a proposal of marriage. (This scene is interesting, too, because Austen changed her mind at the last minute and rewrote the novel's ending, with relatives saving the "canceled" chapters as a curiosity. These are the only draft pages we have of any of Austen's published fiction, and I will discuss what else we can learn from them in the next chapter.) We are very close to the end of *Persuasion* here. A number of characters are gathered in a small public room at Bath, and Captain Wentworth separates himself from the group and sits down to write a letter: "Materials were all at hand, on a separate table," the narrator notes; "he went to it, and nearly turning his back on them all, was engrossed by writing" (*P* II.11, 250). In the meantime, Anne Elliot overhears, inadvertently and rather against her wishes, the details of Henrietta Musgrove's engagement as they are related by Mrs. Musgrove to Mrs. Croft. The women's conversation turns to the undesirability of a long engagement (in other words, an engagement in the absence of some concrete future prospect that would put the couple in a financial position to marry), and when both Mrs. Musgrove and the more worldly-wise Mrs. Croft deplore the phenomenon of the long and uncertain engagement, Anne's attention is captured painfully. The "unexpected interest" she finds here derives from the fact that this consensus would provide unanticipated support for her years-ago decision not to become engaged to Captain Wentworth when he proposed to her without any clear sense of when his financial position would permit them to marry:

> She felt its application to herself, felt it in a nervous thrill all over her, and at the same moment that her eyes instinctively glanced towards the distant table, Captain Wentworth's pen ceased to move, his head was raised, pausing, listening, and he turned round the next instant to give a look—one quick, conscious look at her. (*P* II.11, 251)

That's the first bit of conversation Austen establishes, and then we get a different strand of conversation between Anne and Captain Harville on the topic of love and loss. Captain Benwick, now engaged to Louisa Musgrove, was once engaged to Harville's sister, their engagement broken only by her premature death; Harville has been getting a miniature portrait of Benwick set, originally painted for his sister Fanny but now destined for Louisa. Anne and Captain Harville move on to speak more generally about the longevity of women's love as opposed to men's, with each speaker advocating for his or her own sex, until their exchange is interrupted by "a slight noise" that calls "their attention to Captain Wentworth's hitherto perfectly quiet division of the room. It was nothing more than that his pen had fallen down, but Anne was startled at finding him nearer than she had supposed; and half inclined to suspect that the pen had only fallen, because he had been occupied by them, striving to catch sounds, which yet she did not think he could have caught" (*P* II.11, 254).

In the meantime Captain Harville and Anne conclude their debate, which ends with this concession from Anne: "All the privilege I claim for my own sex (it is not a very enviable one, you need not covet it) is that of loving longest, when existence or when hope is gone" (*P* II.11, 256). Wentworth now seals his letter and leaves in haste, to Anne's distress:

> She had only time, however, to move closer to the table where he had been writing, when footsteps were heard returning; the door opened; it was himself. He begged their pardon, but he had forgotten his gloves, and instantly crossing the room to the writing table, and standing with his back towards Mrs. Musgrove, he drew out a letter from under the scattered paper, placed it before Anne with eyes of glowing entreaty fixed on her for a moment, and hastily collecting his gloves, was again out of the room, almost before Mrs. Musgrove was aware of his being in it—the work of an instant! (*P* II.11, 257)

What Wentworth has given Anne is a brief and passionate written proposal of marriage. Strikingly, then, it is here a letter, not a face-to-face conversation, which provides the greatest and most profoundly transformative experience of intimacy between these two characters: the "conversation" between Anne and Wentworth in the preceding scene is exclusively a matter of trading glances, and it's the letter as powerful personal surrogate that brings these characters finally properly together.

CHAPTER 3

Revision

Looking closely at how Austen revised her own work gives a relatively
clear view of the novelist's writing process, something we can recon-
struct only obliquely from the scraps of historical evidence that survive.
That evidence includes the fair copies Austen made herself, in three
notebooks, of the stories she wrote when she was quite young; a cluster
of unpublished later manuscripts; the letters preserved by family and
friends; and whatever we can extrapolate from the published novels in
the way of hypotheses about technique, story construction, narration
and so forth. Before turning to some of that evidence, though, I want
to look closely at a chunk of textual material I have alluded to already:
the "canceled" chapters of *Persuasion*. As the editors of the Cambridge
edition of *Persuasion* note, "*Persuasion* is unique in having an extant
earlier version of part of its text. All other first drafts of Austen's
completed novels, as well as her final versions, were destroyed ... the
Persuasion fragment exists because it was not printed at the time"
(lxxvii). Austen probably revised the ending to heighten the emotional
intensity of the scene of the proposal discussed at the end of the
previous chapter, but it is fortuitous that the existence of these pages
in manuscript (they were in Cassandra's possession until she died and
then passed down to her niece Anna (lxxxv)) gives us a much clearer
sense than we would have otherwise of what Austen's novel manuscripts probably looked like.

Note especially the extent to which the novels' printers made the choices
about punctuation, capitalization and so forth that lead to the polite and
uniform appearance of the published texts. Austen's own sentences, in the
manuscripts of the letters and in these canceled pages of *Persuasion*, are
spikier, more idiosyncratic than anything we see in her novels as they have
been printed. It is an illusion of sorts, as the sequence of words is identical,
but look at these two versions of the same sentences – the first from an
unpublished chapter in the canceled manuscript, the second as they

actually appeared in print (posthumously, so without the oversight of Austen herself):

> Who can be in doubt of what followed—When any two Young People take it into their heads to marry, they are pretty sure by perseverance to carry their point—be they ever so poor, or ever so imprudent, or ever so little likely to be necessary to each other's ultimate comfort. This may be bad Morality to conclude with, but I beleive it to be Truth—and if such parties succeed, how should a Capt. W——& an Anne E——, with the advantage of maturity of Mind, consciousness of Right, & one Independant Fortune between them, fail of bearing down every opposition? (*P* 322)

And here are the same sentences as they appeared in print:

> Who can be in doubt of what followed? When any two young people take it into their heads to marry, they are pretty sure by perseverance to carry their point, be they ever so poor, or ever so imprudent, or ever so little likely to be necessary to each other's ultimate comfort. This may be bad morality to conclude with, but I believe it to be truth; and if such parties succeed, how should a Captain Wentworth and an Anne Elliot, with the advantage of maturity of mind, consciousness of right, and one independent fortune between them, fail of bearing down every opposition? (*P* II.12, 270)

Spelling and grammar were being standardized over the course of the eighteenth century, and by the early nineteenth century a much more widespread consensus had come into being than had governed the production of printed texts circa 1750, but a passage like this one shows (as do Austen's letters) that Austen in her personal spellings looks backward rather than forward. In this passage, Austen makes two "mistakes" that are still common, having forgotten "i before e except after c" in "believe" and introduced the "a" instead of "e" in "independent." I put the term "mistakes" in scare quotes because they probably didn't register so strongly as such in Austen's time as they would now. They're not so much wrong, in this milieu, as merely not quite the standard dominant spelling. In the canceled chapters, Austen can also be seen to use capitalization for emphasis; there were no strict rules in eighteenth-century English as to what should be capitalized, but it was very common, both in unpublished writing and in printed books, to pick out with a capital any word intended to have more force than its neighbors. I like the rakish, mildly satirical edge of "Young People," which reminds me of Podsnap's fixation in Dickens' great novel *Our Mutual Friend* (1864–65) on whether or not something would "bring a blush into the cheek of the young person," and I believe that looking at these sentences as Austen wrote them, rather than as they were cleaned up for the printed page, heightens appreciation of the satirical edge of so much of Austen's prose.

Richardson's novels offer useful contextual evidence in this regard. The first edition of *Pamela*, published in 1740–41, is full of this kind of capitalization for emphasis, as well as of expressions that are rustic or quaintly provincial, but as Richardson revised for subsequent editions (he was himself a printer who closely oversaw the typesetting of his own novels, so we can make more of the "accidentals" in his novels than we can in those of most of his peers), he cleaned up those expressions, moving in the direction of a more polite and courtly English, as well as increasingly minimizing the use of nonstandard capitalizations, i.e. capitals not at the start of a sentence or for a proper name. Carey McIntosh shows very clearly not just that Richardson's servant heroine Pamela's language is "improved" by her contact with her master Mr. B. – while her language is initially a "rustic idiom" full of dialect phrases and provincial and archaic markers, it becomes more elevated as the story proceeds – but that as Richardson continued to revise the novel for subsequent editions (eight were published during his lifetime), one of his priorities was to make the language less oral, less lower-class and more "polite and genteel."[1] Richardson couldn't leave his own work alone, and though he died before a final set of mark-ups (made during the 1750s) could be transferred into print, that set of edits formed the basis for one final posthumous edition in 1801. If you are curious, you can read this text in the Penguin version of the novel edited by Margaret Doody; it is so different from the first edition (more commonly used as the basis for teaching editions, as it is in Tom Keymer's excellent version for Oxford World's Classics) that they are almost two different novels.

What survives of Austen's early writing doesn't include first drafts. There are fair transcriptions in three notebooks of roughly 74,000 words of fiction, each book bearing a mock title (Volume the First, Volume the Second and Volume the Third) as if the whole collection can be thought of as a three-volume novel, one of the dominant forms of publication for new fiction in this period. These pieces seem to have been composed between the years 1787, when Austen was eleven, and 1793, when she was seventeen (*J* xxiv). Two longer unfinished works also survive in manuscript, *The Watsons* (ca. 1804) and *Sanditon* (1817). The introduction to the Cambridge volume of the *Later Manuscripts* makes a more extended argument for the value of these drafts in terms of what they reveal about Austen's habits of writing and revision, with the editors showing very clearly that while later readers within the family may have felt that the idiosyncrasies of the characters in *Sanditon* should have been toned down, "the revisions show Austen heightening their eccentricities" (lxxxii). Austen's niece Caroline, writing to her brother James Edward Austen-Leigh as he considered which if any of those early fictions to publish alongside a memoir of his aunt, wrote of "Evelyn" that "I have always thought it remarkable that the early workings of her mind should have been in burlesque, and comic exaggeration, setting at nought all rules of probable or possible—when of all her finished and later writings, the exact contrary is the characteristic" (*MJA* 186).

Caroline's assessment may have been a little too simplistic, and elements of burlesque and comic exaggeration can be found even in Austen's last and most somber novel *Persuasion*, but it is a fair point. The first "novel" in the initial volume is strikingly (and successfully) satirical, taking particular advantage of the extent to which compressing a story – speeding up the pace of storytelling – automatically produces the effect of parody. "Frederic and Elfrida, a novel" plays on the absurdity of romance conventions, including but not limited to the sentimentality of much popular fiction, the "novel cant" in which it is couched and the ways characters use that language to justify following their own desires at the expense of external responsibilities and the needs of others, and the sheer absurdity of the trope in which strangers encounter one another and recognize each other as family members (the so-called *coup de sang* or call of blood). This is how the story concludes:

> It was with difficulty that Emma could refrain from tears on hearing of the absence of Edgar; she remained however tolerably composed till the Willmot's were gone when having no check to the overflowings of her greif, she gave free vent to them, and retiring to her own room, continued in tears the remainder of her life. FINIS. (*J* 36–37)

As we might say, THE END!

The early fictions are full of this sort of affectionate mockery of fictional convention. Another one begins by establishing that Sir George and Lady Harcourt's adopted daughter Eliza, in "her eighteenth year . . . happening one day to be detected in stealing a banknote of £50," is "turned out of doors by her inhuman Benefactors" (*J* 38). Note the suggestion that it was the detection of the crime, not the crime itself, that was remarkable: the adjective "inhuman" as applied to her benefactors must derive either from Eliza's own perception or from a partial onlooker, as it is comically at odds with the way an independent observer would be likely to adjudicate fairness. Later in the tale, Eliza's reunion with her adoptive parents prompts her mother to realize that this young woman is not just her adopted daughter but – preposterously, nonsensically – her daughter by birth, as she explains to her husband:

> "Four months after you were gone, I was delivered of this Girl, but dreading your just resentment at her not proving the Boy you wished, I took her to a Haycock and laid her down. A few weeks afterwards, you returned, and fortunately for me, made no enquiries on the subject. Satisfied within myself of the wellfare of my Child, I soon forgot I had one, insomuch that when, we shortly after found her in the very Haycock, I had placed her, I had no more idea of her being my own, than you had, and nothing I will venture to say could have recalled the circumstance to my remembrance, but my thus accidentally hearing her voice which now strikes me as being the very counterpart of my own Child's." (*J* 44)

Similarly, in "Love and Freindship," when a "Gentleman considerably advanced in years" descends from a carriage, romantic letter-writer Laura's "sensibility was wonderfully affected" and she experiences "an instinctive Sympathy . . . that he was my Grandfather":

> Convinced that I could not be mistaken in my conjecture I instantly sprang from the Carriage I had just entered, and following the Venerable Stranger into the Room he had been shewn to, I threw myself on my knees before him and besought him to acknowledge me as his Grand-Child—He started, and after having attentively examined my features, raised me from the Ground and throwing his Grand-fatherly arms around my Neck, exclaimed, "Acknowledge thee! Yes dear resemblance of my Laurina and my Laurina's Daughter, sweet image of my Claudia and my Claudia's Mother, I do acknowledge thee as the Daughter of the one and the Grandaughter of the other." (*J* 120)

As if this were not enough, her friend Sophia comes in search of Laura and is identified by the grandfather as another granddaughter (these names ending in "-a" are typical heroine names), and third and fourth grandchildren enter moments afterward. After establishing that they are the *only* four grandchildren he is likely to discover, the new grandfather gives each young person a fifty-pound note and makes a quick getaway.

This playfulness about the pacing of a story, and in particular the mockery of the abruptness of a certain kind of ending, finds a number of analogies in the published novels. I am thinking especially of the moment near the end of *Northanger Abbey* when the narrator, speaking of the uncertainty as to when Henry and Catherine's engagement will actually culminate in marriage, suggests that their own anxiety about delay "can hardly extend, I fear, to the bosom of my readers, who will see in the tell-tale compression of the pages before them, that we are hastening together to perfect felicity" (*NA* II.16, 259). The joke about the "bookishness" of this kind of storytelling, and the ways in which the number of pages left will give the experienced reader a clue about how close we are to the end, is consistent with the comedy of the juvenilia.

Volume the Second – the notebook is bound in white vellum and bears the inscription "Ex dono mei Patris," a gift of her father's to Austen – has a table of contents that gives titles and pagination, the young writer doing everything she can to give her private production the feel of an actual printed book. This phenomenon can be seen in a host of eighteenth-century drafts and private manuscripts, and shows how pervasive the allure and prestige of print had become even for very young writers – Alexander Pope's early works, for instance, show the poet laboriously and meticulously copying out poems with the layout and appearance of the printed page.[2] Consistent with this kind of self-presentation, Austen's early writings frequently include moments when the author plays with other features of publication: perhaps most notably the dedication, but also a host of the other trappings and appurtenances of real-world publication. "Lesley Castle, an unfinished Novel in Letters" is dedicated to her brother Henry, and below the dedication is a note written by Henry himself – "Messrs Demand and Co—please to pay Jane Austen Spinster the sum of one hundred guineas on account of your Humbl. Servant" (*J* 142; the editor of the Cambridge edition suggests the note might have been added after Henry actually started his bank in 1801, 445 n. 3). In Volume the Third, the longer fiction titled *Catharine, or the Bower* boasts an exuberant dedication to Cassandra:

> Encouraged by your warm patronage of The beautiful Cassandra, and The History of England, which through your generous support, have obtained a place in every library in the Kingdom, and run through threescore Editions, I take the liberty of begging the same Exertions in favour of the following Novel, which I humbly flatter myself, possesses Merit beyond any already published, or any that will ever in future appear, except such as may proceed from the pen of Your Most Grateful Humble Servt.
>
> The Author.
>
> Steventon August 1792 (*J* 241)

It is as though Austen's favorite form of childhood role-playing involved adopting the part of a professional author, though it would be a long wait before she would achieve publication and actually receive payment for her writing.

One of the most fully realized and beautifully executed pieces in the early works must be "The History of England, from the reign of Henry the 4th to the death of Charles the 1st. By a partial, prejudiced, and ignorant Historian" (*J* 176). ("N.B. There will be very few Dates in this History," adds the gleeful historian.) It is a gorgeous manuscript, owned by the British Library and published by them in a facsimile edition that powerfully conveys the history's physical beauty, not least due to the inset colored medallion portraits of the monarchs painted by Cassandra.[3] It is one of those works in which the madcap, self-obsessed voice of certain individual speakers in the novels of Austen's adulthood coalesces most audibly and memorably. Here is the historian's entry for Henry the 6th, quoted in its entirety:

> I cannot say much for this Monarch's Sense—Nor would I if I could, for he was a Lancastrian. I suppose you know all about the Wars between him and the Duke of York who was of the right side; if you do not, you had better read some other History, for I shall not be very diffuse in this meaning by it only to vent my Spleen *against*, and shew my Hatred *to* all those people whose parties or principles do not suit with mine, and not to give information. This King married Margaret of Anjou, a Woman whose distresses and Misfortunes were so great as almost to make me who hate her, pity her. It was in this reign that Joan of Arc lived and made such a *row* among the English. They should not have burnt her—but they did. There were several Battles between the Yorkists and Lancastrians, which the former (as they ought) usually conquered. At length they were entirely over come; The King was murdered—The Queen was sent home—and Edward the 4th Ascended the Throne. (*J* 178)

In contrast to the impartial point of view we might expect a historian to adopt, this historian brandishes his or her monstrous partiality – s/he only admires the party of the Yorkists, despising all Lancastrians regardless of their individual merits and characters, and s/he brazenly challenges the reader who objects to this position to find a different history to read! Giving "information" cannot be the purpose of a righteous historian, after all (we may hear the tongue-in-cheek author behind the voice of the partial historian). After that aside, the historian gives a few cursory facts, none of them phrased in a way that could be helpful to someone wanting a better sense of the period, and then that gruesomely funny and inappropriate aside on Joan of Arc: "They should not have burnt her—but they did." As though the historian has become impatient with his or her own task, the entry ends with comic compression and speeding up so as to get on to the next reign. Austen's pastiche may remind us that even the most apparently objective historian's views will be implicated in partisan positions and beliefs.

The *History of England* is interesting for the light it sheds on Austen's self-involved speakers, but there is also something exciting about it from the point of view of writing process. At some point before she composed this piece and made the fair copy in Volume the Second, a young Jane Austen seems to have written extensive marginalia (more than a hundred comments) in a copy of Oliver Goldsmith's *History of England*.[4] The observations of Goldsmith's that draw the youthful commentator's attention tell us a great deal about Austen's ear for cliché and her debunking orientation toward lazy thinking and critical orthodoxy. When Goldsmith writes "that Cromwell was marching with hasty strides from Scotland," Austen adds in the margin "with his 7 league boots on" (*J* 324). That might just have been a child's silly joke, but in other places in the margins Austen is clearly developing a commenting persona that is related but far from identical to her own self. It is conversational, chatty, often absurd, deeply invested in Tory as opposed to Whig positions.

Goldsmith, reflecting on the behavior of the Whigs during the trial of the Earl of Oxford, writes, "It is, indeed, very remarkable, that all the severe and most restrictive laws were enacted by that party that are continually stunning mankind with a cry of freedom," and Austen comments in the margin: "My dear Dr G—I have lived long enough in the World to know that it is always so!" (*J* 340). And again, extravagantly, on a passage where Goldsmith describes how an act of legislation following the Jacobite rebellion banned the Highland chiefs from wearing the traditional distinctive tartans: "I do not like This—Every ancient custom ought to be sacred unless prejudicial to Happiness" (*J* 351). It almost sounds as though this commentator is echoing and amplifying the conservative voice of Edmund Burke's 1790 *Reflections on the Revolution in France* (Burke was formerly himself a Whig, but sundered himself from the rest of the Whig party when he opposed the early stirrings of the revolution in France). Austen's cousin Eliza's first husband was condemned to death and executed under the Committee of Public Safety in February 1794 (*FR* 77), and though Austen's political opinions are not documented in the historical record, the family was strongly Tory in its sympathies, not least in supporting Warren Hastings (who was cousin Eliza's godfather and a family hero) in the years of his impeachment by Burke and a team of Whig allies for his role as Governor-General of the East India Company.

It's not just bias or partiality that Austen's parody foregrounds. The *History of England* also raises questions about knowledge and its status,

a theme that runs strongly through both the human relationships and the
forms of narration in her later novels. This is how the historian begins the
account of the reign of Henry VIII:

> It would be an affront to my Readers were I to suppose that they were not as
> well acquainted with the particulars of this King's reign as I am myself.
> It will therefore be saving *them* the task of reading again what they have read
> before, and *myself* the trouble of writing what I do not perfectly recollect, by
> giving only a slight sketch of the principal Events which marked his reign.
> (*J* 180)

The entry goes on to note a few largely irrelevant details and provide some
advocacy for Anne Boleyn, then concludes on this wild note: "Tho' I do
not profess giving many dates, yet as I think it proper to give some and shall
of course Make choice of those which it is most necessary for the Reader to
know, I think it right to inform him that her letter to the King was dated on
the 6th of May" (*J* 181). The *year* in which something happened, from the
historian's point of view, will commonly be a more salient fact than the
precise day of the month, and there is a willful comic perversity to
providing the less significant detail even as the more important bit of
information is withheld; the lack of context or specification as to the
letter's contents further underlines the absurdity of the historian's choices.
  Perhaps the climax of the entire piece comes when the historian reaches
the reign of Charles I. Here s/he gives up any pretense of a desire to inform,
pulling aside the veil and revealing the work's true priorities:

> The Events of this Monarch's reign are too numerous for my pen, and
> indeed the recital of any Events (except what I make myself) is uninteresting
> to me; my principal reason for undertaking the History of England being to
> prove the innocence of the Queen of Scotland, which I flatter myself with
> having effectually done, and to abuse Elizabeth, tho' I am rather fearful of
> having fallen short in the latter part of my Scheme. (*J* 188)

The juvenilia offer a good deal of evidence about Austen's priorities and
preferences as a writer of fiction, but we certainly can take some clues from
the letters as well about what sorts of thing caught Austen's attention and
what she liked to make words do in sentences. One taste that comes
through especially clearly is a sharp awareness of infelicities of language,
especially when a sentence would open up an absurd meaning if taken
literally. Here is an example:

> Eliz:th played one Country dance, Lady Bridges the other, which She made
> Henry dance with her; and Miss Finch played the Boulangeries—On read-
> ing over the last three or four Lines, I am aware of my having expressed

myself in so doubtful a manner that if I did not tell you to the contrary, You might imagine it was Lady Bridges who made Henry dance with her, at the same time that she was playing, which if not impossible must appear a very improbable Event to you.—But it was Eliz: who danced—. (*JAL* 8)

And this is another playful example of self-correction in the wake of solecism:

I do not know what is the matter with me to day, but I cannot write quietly; I am always wandering away into some exclamation or other.—Fortunately I have nothing very particular to say.—We walked to Weston one evening last week, & liked it very much.—Liked <u>what</u> very much? Weston?—no— <u>walking</u> to Weston—I have not expressed myself properly, but I hope you will understand me. (*JAL* 47)

Austen begins here very characteristically by reflecting on her own state of mind and current situation (there is no major news to speak of), then segues into the insignificant observation about walking to Weston, which in turn prompts another one of these self-aware self-revisions.

Another revealing kind of commentary in the letters comes when Austen's niece Anna takes up novel-writing and her aunt is invited to comment on chunks of draft pages as Anna sends them to her. Austen's suggestions for revision focus strongly around questions of realism and verisimilitude; this is the same decade that would see Coleridge coining the phrase "willing suspension of disbelief," and it is clear that Austen understands how delicate the immersion of reader into fictional reality may be, and how easily the illusion of reality can be broken by an improbable detail. When she writes with irritation about another novel she's reading that "[t]here are a thousand improbabilities in the story" (*JAL* 301), it's worth noting that the term "probable" had more weight than it does for us now, carrying some of the flavor of "plausible" and some of the force of "possible" but with a very strong root sense of being provable, or of existing in the world of evidence and corroboration.[5]

Here are Austen's comments on an initial batch of Anna's pages:

A few verbal corrections were all that I felt tempted to make—the principal of them is a speech of St. Julians to Lady Helena—which you will see I have presumed to alter.—As Lady H. is Cecilia's superior, it wd not be correct to talk of <u>her</u> being introduced; Cecilia must be the person introduced—And I do not like a Lover's speaking in the 3d person; it is too much like the formal part of Lord Orville, & I think it is not natural. (*JAL* 278)

These criticisms rely on Austen's nuanced and highly textural sense both of literary style and of social manners and interactions. A sort of "fact-checking" mentality is constantly running just below the surface of her reading, and when Anna asks her aunt to be particularly attentive in her evaluation of the novel's representation of a town called Dawlish, Austen writes:

> I am not sensible of any Blunders about Dawlish. The Library was particularly pitiful & wretched 12 years ago, & not likely to have anybody's publication.—There is no such Title as Desborough—either among the Dukes, Marquisses, Earls, Viscounts or Barons. (*JAL* 279)

The criteria that Anna and her aunt care about prioritize the creation of a pervasive "reality effect," a phrase Roland Barthes coined in a somewhat different context.[6] If a novel tells us that a character can't find a recent publication at the library, this will only make sense if the library referred to is known to be fairly inadequate; the fiction must be anchored in specific times and places, or the representation will not remain probable. We know that Austen exerted a very similar kind of scrutiny on her own fiction, as when she notes in a letter (it is during the period in which she is composing *Mansfield Park*) that "I learn from Sir J. Carr that there is no Government House at Gibraltar.—I must alter it to the Commissioner's" (*JAL* 207). Anna also presumably wishes to avoid using the name of a real member of the nobility, and has asked her aunt to double-check that "Desborough" is available for her to assign to a purely fictional character. Very strict defamation laws in England during this period meant that authors had to be extremely careful not to implicate real historical figures in their stories; beyond that, though, it also can produce a break in plausibility if the name of a character in a novel is identical to that of someone who gets a good deal of attention in real life.

The realistic texture of Austen's fiction is highly dependent on the author's attention to factual detail and social nuance. In a letter that succeeds this one, she writes tactfully to Anna as follows:

> My Corrections have not been more important than before; here & there, we have thought the sense might be expressed in fewer words—and I have scratched out Sir Tho: from walking with the other Men to the Stables &c the very day after his breaking his arm—for though I find your Papa <u>did</u> walk out immediately after <u>his</u> arm was set, I think it can be so little usual as to <u>appear</u> unnatural in a book–& it does not seem to be material that Sir Tho: should go with them. (*JAL* 280)

This kind of consideration also underpins some of her other suggestions, so that Austen writes a little later, "your aunt C. & I both recommend your making a little alteration in the last scene between Devereux F. & Lady

Clanmurray & her Daughter. We think they press him too much—more than sensible Women or well-bred Women would do." As she continues to comment on successive installments, Austen offers further criticisms (more, the aunt says, than the niece "will like"):

> We are not satisfied with Mrs F.'s settling herself as Tenant & near Neighbour to such a Man as Sir T. H. without having some other induce-ment to go there; she ought to have some friend living thereabouts to tempt her. A woman, going with two girls just growing up, into a Neighbourhood where she knows nobody but one Man, of not very good character, is an awkwardness which so prudent a woman as Mrs F. would not be likely to fall into. Remember, she is very prudent;—you must not let her act incon-sistently. (*JAL* 286)

The scenario here is rather reminiscent of the opening of *Sense and Sensibility*, but the more important point is that characters must behave consistently (Fielding's name for the principle was "conservation of char-acter") – if we are to believe in them, the rationales that motivate their choices and actions mustn't contradict the other traits and qualities the fiction assigns to them, or else the reading experience will become non-sensical. That said, detail shouldn't be too fully rendered, or it detracts from the reader's enjoyment: "You describe a sweet place, but your descriptions are often more minute than will be liked," Austen tells Anna elsewhere. "You give too many particulars of right hand & left.—" (*JAL* 287).

Matters of phrasing – and a dislike for cliché and "novel jargon" or "novel slang" – also prompt criticism. At one point, Austen objects to Anna letting her protagonist "plunge into a 'vortex of Dissipation'": "I do not object to the Thing," she adds, "but I cannot bear the expression; it is such thorough novel slang—and so old, that I dare say Adam met with it in the first novel he opened" (*JAL* 289). This moment might remind us of a few words Willoughby utters to Elinor during his visit to the house where Marianne lies ill, about how he felt when he received Marianne's first letter:

> "Every line, every word was—in the hackneyed metaphor which their dear writer, were she here, would forbid—a dagger to my heart. To know that Marianne was in town was—in the same language—a thunderbolt.— Thunderbolts and daggers!—what a reproof would she have given me!— her taste, her opinions—I believe they are better known to me than my own,—and I am sure they are dearer." (*SS* III.8, 368)

The problem with this kind of metaphor isn't just that it's overused but that it is so generic. It erases the particularity of one person's feelings and makes them like every other person's experience of a similar thing, which may be the emotional reality of life (we often fall into cliché in times of great emotional turmoil) but is not the mode of good writing.

It is in this series of letters to Anna that we find the passage so often quoted as a description of Austen's own craft: "You are now collecting your People delightfully, getting them exactly into such a spot as is the delight of my life," she writes; "3 or 4 Families in a Country Village is the very thing to work on" (*JAL* 287). And another piece of advice to Anna also speaks very directly to the choices Austen made in her own fiction concerning what kinds of people and settings to represent. "[W]e think you had better not leave England," she tells Fanny (Cassandra is the other reader whose verdicts Austen transmits). "Let the Portmans go to Ireland, but as you know nothing of the Manners there, you had better not go with them. You will be in danger of giving false representations. Stick to Bath & the Foresters. There you will be quite at home" (*JAL* 280–81).

There are writers whose manuscripts have survived in such quantities that there is a good deal of direct evidence as to their habits of composition and practices of revision: Alexander Pope would be a good example of this kind. But where the evidence is slighter, as in Austen's case, we make what we can of the evidence we have. Verbal tradition within the Austen family is often the chief source of information about major projects of composition and revision: so as to say, the project that would be published in 1811 as *Sense and Sensibility* was probably first written as an epistolary novel called *Elinor and Marianne* in 1795, revised with third-person narration under the new title *Sense and Sensibility* in 1797 and revised again in 1809–10 with a view toward publication. This is useful to know partly because it accounts for the formal traces of epistolarity treated in the chapter on letters, but also because some striking traces of 1790s issues and debates can still be discerned in the version of a decade later, a fact that in turn suggests we may understand more about Austen's choices and goals in *Sense and Sensibility* if we put it in the context of the Jacobin and anti-Jacobin novels of a decade and a half earlier (*SS* xxiii).

Sometimes even meager evidence about Austen's writing habits, too, can give us a way to understand something about the near-miraculous formal perfection of her greatest novels. *Pride and Prejudice* is a masterpiece of construction and economy, beautifully pieced together with the elegance and symmetry of something like Mozart's *Così fan Tutte*; perhaps even more so, *Persuasion* has not a single wasted word in it. But for me the most supreme artistry of construction in all of Austen's fiction can be found in *Emma*, and I will spend the last bit of this chapter showing some of the ways in which what we do know about choices Austen made in earlier works, some published and some not, can provide illuminating contexts for the techniques and mechanisms of the mature fiction.

Emma is built around puzzles, with Austen inviting us early on in the novel to think about the structural properties of riddles, charades and the like, as well as what it is we do when we decode them. Emma's friend Harriet Smith has undertaken a project (the sort of amusement considered suitable for young women during this period) to collect and transcribe riddles "into a thin quarto of hot-pressed paper, made up by her friend [i.e., Emma], and ornamented with cyphers and trophies" (*E* I.9, 74). Mr. Elton, who has been paying a great deal of attention to Emma and her friend, composes a charade for inclusion in the volume: this takes the form of a poem whose first stanza consists of two couplets, each of which offers a smaller riddle whose answer is a single word ("court," "ship"), and whose second stanza gives the clue to combine the two words into a single key: "courtship." This kind of charade was popular in the period, and we have textual evidence that Austen liked to write charades for family entertainment: there is one in the *History of England* (*J* 187), and three independent ones survive in the collection of later manuscripts.

Jan Marsh, writing about Christina Rossetti's *bouts rimés* (poems produced in response to a list of rhymed words, each of which has to come in the correct order as the final word of the line), observes that texts produced by this sort of rapid composition "are almost in the nature of automatic writing, their themes were always prompted by the rhyme words, and although generally dismissed as insignificant compositions, they reflect very present concerns."[7] Austen's charades have some of the same quality, their ad hoc nature revealing preoccupations and concerns taken up more substantively elsewhere in the fiction. I find a little uncanny the extent to which these early charades of Austen's actually anticipate and delineate the themes of the later fiction. Here is one:

> When my 1st is a task to a young girl of spirit
> And my second confines her to finish the piece
> How hard is her fate! But how great is her merit
> If by taking my whole she effect her release!   (*LM* 256)

The "hem" is the task, and the "lock" is the mechanism that confines her to finish her sewing, an emblem of domestic constraints that is literalized in the second word; the key to the whole riddle is "hemlock," the poison taken by Socrates to commit suicide, and the madcap jaunty charade suggests that suicide might indeed be the only release from this sort of

plight. This is a playful rather than a serious suggestion, obviously – Austen
was an orthodox Christian, a sincere believer who would in no context have
condoned suicide, which was a sin according to the canons of the church.

The second of the two I give here is perhaps even more suggestive of the
plots of novels like *Mansfield Park* and *Persuasion*:

> You may lie on my first, by the side of a stream,
> And my second compose to the Nymph you adore
> But if when you've none of my whole, her esteem
> And affection diminish, think of her no more.

It is a "bank" that we lie on beside the stream, and a "note" that we write to
our loved one (the addressee here is male): the second couplet tells him that
if he doesn't have any "banknotes" and his loved one's affection
diminishes, he must dismiss her from his mind.

Back to the riddle Mr. Elton offers to the ladies in *Emma*: Emma
decodes it instantly, while Harriet is comically slow and maladroit to
follow its insinuations, but then Emma herself more fundamentally mis-
reads the underlying message. As she says to herself later on, that final
couplet – "Thy ready wit the word will soon supply, / May its approval
beam in that soft eye" – sounds like a muddled hybrid of Emma and
Harriet, with "ready wit" not really applicable to the latter and "soft eye"
inapposite for the former. The novel also contains a larger riddle that
Emma fails to solve till very late in the novel, though she identifies its
existence when she calls Jane Fairfax "a riddle, quite a riddle" (*E* II.15, 307).
Austen cleverly points us to the centrality of this riddle (and to Emma's
failure to understand its dimensions) by elsewhere elaborating these tropes
of riddles, puzzles and so forth. Scholarly editions and annotation are
another form of puzzle-solving that would have been familiar to Austen
and her circle: over the course of the eighteenth century, Shakespeare
editions proliferated, many of them making heavy use of the technique
of textual emendation. This involved finding places in the text that didn't
make sense, then showing how factors like printers' errors, glitches from
combining different editions and so forth might have produced those local
pockets of incomprehensibility, and finally suggesting a new possibility (an
"emendation") consistent with the text's underlying rationale that would
make more sense in context. At one point early in the novel, Emma,
bumptiously delighted by the love matches that seem to be forming around
her, quotes the Shakespeare line "The course of true love never did run
smooth—" (*E* I.9, 80), from *A Midsummer Night's Dream*, but only as
a negative example: "A Hartfield edition of Shakespeare would have a long

note on that passage," she adds smugly. Typical editorial annotation of this era touched not just on textual questions but on the moral and psychological truth or otherwise of the author's sentiments, and annotation joins other kinds of riddle-solving in the annals of Highbury.

It's not just the thematic emphasis on riddles that becomes clearer if we contextualize it with Austen's interest and practice as a historical reader and writer. Perhaps the most striking thing about *Emma* is that it reads completely differently the second time round. Clues as to the secret underlying story – the one we learn about at the novel's end, and that will inform our subsequent rereadings – are so subtly placed that they are genuinely invisible the first time through and will remain indeterminate thereafter, by which I mean to say that I still often can't decide, even after repeated rounds of rereading, whether the narrator at a given point "knows" the secret or not. In this sense *Emma* the novel both recapitulates and builds on a narrative strategy Austen tried out in *Northanger Abbey*.

Let me first describe how this structure works in the later novel. The secret – this is a spoiler, and if you haven't read *Emma* you might prefer to jump to the beginning of the next chapter – is that Frank Churchill, known to be unattached and projected by all to be Emma's prospective husband, has actually been engaged to Jane Fairfax since well before we first meet him at Highbury. Emma knows that Jane has met Frank, and would love to learn more about him. Already irritated by Jane's reticence, though, Emma as she attempts to gain information bumps up against Jane's immense reserve (the narrator may be quoting Jane's own words in the first sentence here, or rather paraphrasing them): "She and Mr. Frank Churchill had been at Weymouth at the same time. It was known that they were a little acquainted; but not a syllable of real information could Emma procure as to what he truly was" (*E* II.2, 181). Emma has no suspicion, however, that anything other than general reserve motivates Jane's reticence, nor, when she meets Frank a few chapters later and asks him whether he saw Jane much when they were both at Weymouth, does she manage to detect what upon *re*-reading we surely must identify as a dodge:

> At this moment they were approaching Ford's, and he hastily exclaimed, "Ha! This must be the very shop that every body attends every day of their lives, as my father informs me . . . If it be not inconvenient to you, pray let us go in, that I may prove myself to belong to the place, to be a true citizen of Highbury. I must buy something at Ford's. It will be taking out my free-dom.—I dare say they sell gloves." (*E* II.6, 215)

("Freedom" here isn't synonymous with liberty; it refers playfully to the "freedom of the city," an honor a municipality might bestow on a local pillar of the community or a visiting dignitary.)

Only once they have asked to see some gloves does Frank revisit Emma's question, which she must repeat to him first. She asks him again whether he "had known much of Miss Fairfax and her party at Weymouth," and he now answers as follows (the interval has presumably given him time to collect his thoughts):

> "And now that I understand your question, I must pronounce it to be a very unfair one. It is always the lady's right to decide on the degree of acquaintance. Miss Fairfax must already have given her account.—I shall not commit myself by claiming more than she may chuse to allow." (*E* II.6, 216)

On first reading, this is merely playful. Only on a second reading, and in light of what we learn at the novel's conclusion, does Frank's answer come to sound deliberately disingenuous.

The novel continues to be structured around a series of riddles or puzzles: there is the piano Jane Fairfax receives from an unknown benefactor (*E* II.8, 232) and the mystery of why Frank goes to London on the spur of the moment to get his hair cut; there is the scene where Frank stares at Jane at a party and tells Emma he is going to talk to her, with the added twist that though he tells Emma to look and see how she takes the impertinent question he threatens to ask Jane, in fact, "as to its effect on the young lady, as he had improvidently placed himself exactly between them, exactly in front of Miss Fairfax, she could absolutely distinguish nothing" (*E* II.8, 240). There is Frank's readiness to promise visits to Jane's aunt Miss Bates (*E* II.9, 252) and to find pretexts for additional visits, as in the case where he says he is going to return a borrowed pair of scissors (*E* III.3, 361). Frank himself suspects that all of this may have revealed his secret to Emma, and at the end of volume two (Austen, like many of her peers, makes use of fixed printer's divisions to structure her story and heighten its effects), he visits her at home and tells her she must "hardly be quite without suspicion" (*E* II.12, 281) – but she cuts him off, thinking he may be about to propose to her, and the opportunity to reveal his secret and perhaps enlist Emma as an ally is lost.

The larger puzzle structure the novel's built around has an earlier analog, as I have suggested, whose more rudimentary construction helps us better understand how the later one works and why it might have been put together. *Northanger Abbey* was only published after Austen died, but an earlier version of the text was substantially complete by 1800 and was sold under the name *Susan*, after which point the publisher (it must have been immensely frustrating for the aspiring novelist) would then neither print it nor sell the copyright back to the author. The striking commonality here concerns the way that the narrator notes and delineates a series of exchanges and encounters that cannot be decoded by the first-time reader but that serve as a series of "clues" for the plot's central mechanism and open themselves up to comprehension only on rereading. It is a simple plot. Catherine Morland is taken up by the ambitious General Tilney as a possible marriage partner for his younger son; although her portion is actually moderate, he has been misinformed, believing her to possess great expectations to the extent of being an heiress. When he finds out the truth, he sends Catherine home in a rage, the event serving as a sort of domestic parody of the kinds of danger that the heroines of gothic novels typically fall into, although Claudia L. Johnson persuasively suggests that *Northanger Abbey* is a genuinely "alarming" novel insofar as it domesticates gothic elements in order to show that paternal figures can be dangerous not just in continental castles of days gone by but in contemporary England as well.[8]

This is almost a mock-heroic plot; the gothic has been transmuted into a reassuringly ordinary setting, and the novel will have a happy ending. The backstory that will need to be clarified, though, involves the novel providing a detailed and rational explanation for how the initial conditions of misinformation could have come about. It is clever but crude; we see the "seams" of the construction. Early on, Catherine sees her friend Isabella's brother John Thorpe "engaged in conversation with General Tilney"; "and she felt something more than surprise," the narrator adds, "when she thought she could perceive herself the object of their attention and discourse" (*NA* I.12, 94). But it is an inconsequential detail in a flurry of seemingly more salient information, and it is only in the unfolding of secrets at the end that we understand what happened. General Tilney has thrown Catherine out of the house not because he has discovered in her some form of moral turpitude, but on account of his uncontrolled rage at having been misinformed to his own disadvantage:

> The General had had nothing to accuse her of, nothing to lay to her charge, but her being the involuntary, unconscious object of a deception which his pride could not pardon, and which a better pride would have been ashamed to own. She was guilty only of being less rich than he had supposed her to be. Under a mistaken persuasion of her possessions and claims, he had courted her acquaintance in Bath, solicited her company at Northanger, and designed her for his daughter in law. (*NA* II.15, 253)

And then the backstory, the "re-narration" of an incident we saw and noted the first time (with Catherine and the narrator) without understanding its significance:

> John Thorpe had first misled him. The General, perceiving his son one night at the theatre to be paying considerable attention to Miss Morland, had accidentally inquired of Thorpe, if he knew more of her than her name. Thorpe, most happy to be on speaking terms with a man of General Tilney's importance, had been joyfully and proudly communicative;—and being at that time not only in daily expectation of Morland's engaging Isabella, but likewise pretty well resolved upon marrying Catherine himself, his vanity induced him to represent the family as yet more wealthy than his vanity and avarice had made him believe them. With whomsoever he was, or was likely to be connected, his own consequence always required that theirs should be great, and as his intimacy with any acquaintance grew, so regularly grew their fortune. (*NA* II.15, 254)

This sort of outright demystification has come to seem dispensable by the time Austen writes *Emma*, and the greater subtlety and the more delicate elaboration of the central puzzle in *Emma* are striking in contrast. The key clue in the later novel is given in one great long anomalous scene – anomalous because we see it from the point of view of Mr. Knightley rather than through Emma's eyes – where Frank betrays knowledge of the idea of Mr. Perry setting up his carriage, an idea known only to a handful of people before a change of heart rendered the information no longer correct.[9] We later deduce that Frank must have had this information in a letter from Jane, who would have heard it from her aunt (we know that the plan was known to Miss Bates), but Frank preposterously suggests that he must have imagined it in a dream, a suggestion that provokes Mr. Knightley's suspicion. Frank in the meantime is trying to catch Jane's eye and Jane is evading his gaze, signs of communication that only increase the watcher's suspicion, and the scene culminates in a moment we witness with Mr. Knightley, one that incredibly powerfully combines the novel's emphasis on limitations of knowledge and on riddles and their solutions.

The company are playing a game of anagrams or letter scramble with the alphabet Emma has made for her nephews to play with, and this is the exchange Knightley witnesses:

> Frank Churchill placed a word before Miss Fairfax. She gave a slight glance round the table, and applied herself to it. Frank was next to Emma, Jane opposite to them—and Mr. Knightley so placed as to see them all; and it was his object to see as much as he could, with as little apparent observation.

The word was discovered, and with a faint smile pushed away. If meant to be immediately mixed with the others, and buried from sight, she should have looked on the table instead of looking just across, for it was not mixed; and Harriet, eager after every fresh word, and finding out none, directly took it up, and fell to work. She was sitting by Mr. Knightley, and turned to him for help. The word was *blunder*; and as Harriet exultingly proclaimed it, there was a blush on Jane's cheek which gave it a meaning not otherwise ostensible. Mr. Knightley connected it with the dream; but how it could all be, was beyond his comprehension. (*E* III.5, 377)

The first-level meaning of the word is simple, but it's the second-level meaning (or the witnessing of the exchange of meaning) that brings the blush to Jane's cheek and gives it that "meaning not otherwise ostensible."

In a final touch that again shows the delicacy of Austen's fictional technique at this stage of her writing career, near the end of the scene "Mr. Knightley thought he saw another collection of letters anxiously pushed towards her, and resolutely swept away by her unexamined" (*E* III.5, 379). The novel never tells us what that word might have been. It is a pocket of inscrutability, though we understand that the important piece of knowledge here concerns simply the fact of communication. (Appealingly a family tradition has it that the word was "pardon" (*MJA* 119).) By juxtaposing comparable sequences in the two novels, then, we learn something important about how and why knowledge interacts with forms of narration, and individual novel pairings around a specific problem of character, plot or narration will frequently help the reader develop a coherent and persuasive critical take on how to interpret any given choice of Austen's.

CHAPTER 4

Manners

"Politeness," "civility," "punctilio": Austen has a number of different words for manners, each one with slightly different connotations, and many of the things she's interested in about human interaction fall under manners as a broad rubric, insofar as that term covers the deeper as well as more superficial ways people treat one another in company. *Sense and Sensibility* is the novel of Austen's that argues most aggressively for how much weight civility must bear as it shades into subtler, more elusive qualities like self-command and self-control. The system of manners the novel puts forward constitutes a crucial shared framework for values and behavior, and each inflection of manners Austen depicts reveals a different set of commitments around identity, intimacy and community. At one point early on, with Marianne Dashwood and Willoughby already very taken with each other, Elinor Dashwood overhears Willoughby telling her sister that even if she can't accept a horse from him now (their mother has nowhere to stable it, and it is both an inappropriately costly present and a gift that would lock Marianne's family in on an ongoing expense they can't afford), the animal in question now belongs to her and will be hers in reality when she leaves Barton "to form [her] own establishment in a more lasting home": "and in the whole of the sentence," the narrator continues,

> in his manner of pronouncing it, and in his addressing her sister by her Christian name alone, she instantly saw an intimacy so decided, a meaning so direct, as marked a perfect agreement between them. From that moment she doubted not of their being engaged to each other; and the belief of it created no other surprise, than that she, or any of their friends, should be left by tempers so frank, to discover it by accident. (*SS* I.12, 70)

Elinor isn't making an unwarranted assumption. She shares with the society in which she lives a high degree of commitment to politeness and its protocols, and the novel suggests that it is eminently reasonable for her to take this verbal exchange as evidence that an engagement must exist between Willoughby and her sister.

The only puzzle, as she sees it, is that she and her mother have not been apprised of it explicitly. When their younger sister says she has seen Willoughby cut off a lock of Marianne's hair, kiss it, fold it up in a piece of paper and place it in his pocketbook, they all feel they have enough evidence to be sure (*SS* I.12, 71). But why, given the couple's commitment to sincerity, haven't they told Marianne's closest family members? Mrs. Dashwood is upset that Elinor seems to doubt the engagement, but as Elinor responds, "every circumstance except *one* is in favour of their engagement; but that *one* is the total silence of both on the subject, and with me it almost outweighs every other" (*SS* I.15, 93). Marianne has embraced the doctrine of perfect transparency and openness that is associated with philosopher Jean-Jacques Rousseau and his followers (political philosopher and novelist William Godwin was one of its best-known English proponents), and *Sense and Sensibility* pits the two sisters' divergent systems of manners and values against each other, judging the mode of sincerity generally more selfish and less socially responsible than the kinds of polite dissimulation that protect others and that sometimes even help us protect ourselves from the damage caused by our own uncontrolled feelings. That said, the novel detects high costs for women in both modes of manners, and it is by no means clear that sense trumps sensibility as a path to true fulfillment; it can be considered more in light of a survival strategy than as a positive good in its own right.

Politeness governs not just what we say and how we should speak to one another but also our behavior in a more general sense, with "propriety" being one of the names we give to what we consider right and appropriate. The difference between politeness and propriety is a subtle one; in some contexts, it may be merely a fine distinction of nomenclature, but we could think of politeness as motivated mostly by concern for others and propriety as motivated more by concern for one's reputation. In this sense, propriety can easily be stigmatized as foolish convention, particularly when it involves double standards of behavior for men and for women (as it certainly does in Austen's novels), and yet in many contexts Austen's novels celebrate propriety as socially essential. Both the negative and the positive views of propriety are grounded in reality, though which aspect we choose to emphasize will depend on our identifications and roles in society.

Elinor is distressed to learn that Marianne has gone with Willoughby to visit his elderly relative's house while she is in residence there but without being introduced to her; Marianne offers the rebuttal that as the visit was very pleasant, it must therefore have been right. When Elinor then suggests "that the pleasantness of an employment does not always evince its propriety," Marianne demurs: "On the contrary, nothing can be a stronger proof of it, Elinor, for if there had been any real impropriety in what I did, I should have been sensible of it at the time, for we always know when we are acting wrong, and with such a conviction I could have had no pleasure" (*SS* II.13, 80). Marianne hasn't drawn this doctrine out of thin air: it is a watered-down version of what was often called "moral sense" philosophy, a school of thought that originates most clearly in Shaftesbury's precept that feelings are the best test of whether something is right or wrong and that was developed further by David Hume, Francis Hutcheson, Adam Smith and others over the century that followed. Skepticism about the basic premise might derive, as I think it does here, from the pragmatic suspicion that doing the right thing is often likely to feel difficult or distressing. It is also potentially related to a strain of argument (one current in our own society as well) about the dangers of considering feelings of affirmation or repulsion as a test of morality; the feeling of visceral disgust has not been a particularly trustworthy guide to moral behavior over the years, and it always risks toppling over into xenophobia and other forms of damaging prejudice.

One of Elinor's strongest commitments in the field of propriety involves a refusal to express negative feelings externally. She hews to a self-imposed ban on revealing any lowness of spirits in her outward demeanor, partly as a matter of self-protection but also so as not to trigger the concern of others. When Edward Ferrars' visit ends on a low note that calls into question their growing closeness, Elinor feels sad, but she is also determined to subdue that feeling, a choice the narrator seems to endorse. Refraining from adopting "the method so judiciously employed by Marianne, on a similar occasion, to augment and fix her sorrow, by seeking silence, solitude, and idleness," we learn, Elinor keeps herself busy, neither seeking nor avoiding mention of Edward's name:

> and if, by this conduct, she did not lessen her own grief, it was at least prevented from unnecessary increase, and her mother and sisters were spared much solicitude on her account. Such behaviour as this, so exactly the reverse of her own, appeared no more meritorious to Marianne, than her own had seemed faulty to her. The business of self-command she settled very easily;—with strong affections it was impossible, with calm ones it could have no merit. That her sister's affections *were* calm, she dared not deny, though she blushed to acknowledge it; and of the strength of her own, she gave a very striking proof, by still loving and respecting that sister, in spite of this mortifying conviction. (*SS* I.19, 120–21)

There is something polemical about the position-taking here, perhaps not surprising in a novel that had its roots in the 1790s and was partly inspired by Britain's wild cultural and political polarizations in the wake of revolution in France. The novel comes down strongly on the side of self-control and dissimulation – or does it? The arguments of Austen's novels are often tricky to pin down. Claudia L. Johnson has emphasized that despite Elinor and Marianne existing at the two far poles of an orientation toward concealment, they suffer very similar fates: in her words, "Elinor's behavior has turned out to differ from Marianne's only in degree and not in kind" (*Jane Austen: Women, Politics and the Novel,* 63).

It is possible that Elinor's desire to protect herself from unwanted feelings tips her too far over to the side of politeness. When she is overwhelmed by the professions of outrage made by friends and family concerning the news of Willoughby's engagement to a woman who is not Marianne, Elinor finds a decorous silence (however cold) preferable to the warmth of real sympathy:

> The calm and polite unconcern of Lady Middleton on the occasion was an happy relief to Elinor's spirits, oppressed as they often were by the clamorous kindness of the others. It was a great comfort to her, to be sure of exciting no interest in *one* person at least among their circle of friends; a great comfort to know that there was *one* who would meet her without feeling any curiosity after particulars, or any anxiety for her sister's health.
>
> Every qualification is raised at times, by the circumstances of the moment, to more than its real value; and she was sometimes worried down by officious condolence to rate good-breeding as more indispensable to comfort than good-nature. (*SS* II.10, 245)

The tone of the first paragraph is sincere rather than ironic, I would say: it really is "a great comfort" to Elinor not to have to respond politely to yet another set of expressions of outrage and sympathy. But the narrative tone shifts in the second paragraph, offering a less partial commentary on how the particular context may have biased Elinor unreasonably against good nature and in the direction of good breeding. The reader will suspect that the narrator too ranks good nature above good breeding, and yet the willfully teeter-tottering nature of Austen's arguments doesn't leave that assertion uncomplicated.

Consider this passage later in the novel (Mrs. Palmer is Lady Middleton's sister, and the two represent complementary and equally radical distortions of manners):

> Nothing was wanting on Mrs. Palmer's side that constant and friendly good-humour could do, to make them feel themselves welcome.

> The openness and heartiness of her manner, more than atoned for that want
> of recollection and elegance, which made her often deficient in the forms of
> politeness; her kindness, recommended by so pretty a face, was engaging;
> her folly, though evident, was not disgusting, because it was not conceited;
> and Elinor could have forgiven every thing but her laugh. (*SS* III.6, 344)

This suggests that even intellectual or ethical acceptance of certain
kinds of manners may bump up against an irreducible bulwark of
taste, something that exists more in the realm of aesthetics than ethics
but is no less fundamental for that reason. *Sense and Sensibility* offers
an exhaustive catalog of different kinds of bad manners: the vulgarity
of Mrs. Jennings, the cold snobbery of Mrs. John Dashwood, the
man-obsession of Miss Steele and Lucy Steele's unmitigated pursuit of
her own self-interest, the elder Mrs. Ferrars' controlling behavior and
rudeness to Elinor, even Mr. Robert Ferrars' preference for choosing
a toothpick case over ceding his place to the ladies who are waiting to
be served.

Contrary to the impression that may be left by the novels as a whole,
perhaps even more so by many of the film adaptations, the social milieu of
Austen's own life, centering on the parsonage at Steventon where her father
held the living, was made up of families with a more precarious hold on
gentility than most of the fictional ones she depicts. "A steady, backbone-of-
England, unchanging rural society is what you expect to find," writes
Austen's biographer Claire Tomalin; "but the strange fact is that they formed
a very unstable group, and that many were what has been called in this
century pseudo-gentry, families who aspired to live by the values of the
gentry without owning land or inherited wealth of any significance. There
were remarkably few Dashwoods or Darcys, Bertrams, Rushworths or
Elliots; Bingley's uncertainty about where he belonged and where he
might settle comes much closer to them" (87).

In later chapters I'll draw on other materials from Austen's life to round
out our sense of the social world she depicts in the novels, but I will note
here that the letters are full of funny details that touch on the author's own
personal relationship to the protocols of politeness, as well as to the
pleasures and penalties of other people's company. It is clear that people,
their foibles and the ins and outs of their social interactions are Austen's
chief interest in life as in art. She has a strong preference for watching
people as opposed to visiting museums and galleries, where "my preference
for Men & Women," as she says, "always inclines me to attend more to the
company than the sight" (*JAL* 187). It pleases Austen to affect a slightly
misanthropic voice in the letters, and there is a good deal of ambivalence

about some of the forms of sociability she is forced to undergo: "Miss Blachford is agreeable enough," she writes; "I do not want People to be very agreeable, as it saves me the trouble of liking them a great deal" (*JAL* 30). The demands of sociability particularly attract her opprobrium: "We are to have a tiny party here tonight; I hate tiny parties—they force one into constant exertion.—"

At many moments in the letters, Austen expresses a considerable sensitivity to differentials of money and social capital, especially as they are experienced by the recipients of others' condescension or largesse. The word "condescension" has for us a mostly disparaging sense, but the late eighteenth century was witnessing a tug-of-war between an older sense, in which "condescension" wasn't a negative term but only appropriately described the manner of superiors toward their social inferiors, and a new awareness of such complacency about social difference as itself having become anachronistic or obnoxious, with condescension now signaling the inappropriate and unwanted show of generosity from individuals whose feeling of social superiority is not recognized as valid or relevant. Being habitually in a position of poverty and dependency can induce a certain defensiveness. Some of Austen's relatives were much better off than others, with one brother adopted into a wealthier childless branch of the family and several other brothers marrying into money, and one or two of the sisters-in-law showed some insensitivity to how their hospitality or lack thereof may have made a husband's dependent sisters feel.

Visiting her wealthy aunt in Bath, Austen reflects on the awkwardness of being a poor relation: "My Aunt is in a great hurry to pay me for my Cap, but cannot find in her heart to give me good money," she writes to Cassandra. "'If I have any intention of going to the Grand Sydney-Garden Breakfast, if there is any party I wish to join, Perrot will take out a ticket for me.'—Such an offer I shall of course decline; & all the service she will render me therefore, is to put it out of my power to go at all, whatever may occur to make it desirable" (*JAL* 107–08). Austen often enough felt the sting of being neglected because of a perceived lack of status that a certain preemptive defensiveness (perhaps we could call it self-protective cynicism) creeps into her feelings about meeting new people. When Austen and her brother Francis pay a visit to one Mrs. Lance, for instance, the lady "is civil and chatty enough, and offered to introduce us to some acquaintance in Southampton, which we gratefully declined"; the adjective "gratefully" may have a slight hint of irony, as the thought that follows is considerably more cynical:

I suppose they must be acting by the orders of Mr. Lance of Netherton in this civility, as there seems no other reason for their coming near us. They will not come often, I dare say. They live in a handsome style and are rich, and she seemed to like to be rich, and we gave her to understand that we were far from being so; she will soon feel therefore that we are not worth her acquaintance. (*JAL* 122)

We are especially well primed to identify failures of civility in those we concede to be our superiors (a boss, a wealthy older relative, an exceptionally attractive love object, the waiter at a very expensive restaurant). A more cynical extension of this would be to say that almost everyone will fail in civility when their manners are truly seen and known, and the premise that manners are perceived most clearly from below is encapsulated in the eighteenth-century saying that "No man is a hero to his valet de chambre." Even as a very young writer, Austen has begun to make the kind of pointed social observation that will be so successfully integrated into the novels of her adulthood. I like this example from one of the fictional letters in the piece in the juvenilia called "A Collection of Letters" (it represents a series of self-contained experiments in voice and storytelling rather than a unified longer story):

The next day while we were at dinner Lady Greville's Coach stopped at the door, for that is the time of day she generally contrives it should. She sent in a message by the Servant to say that "she should not get out but that Miss Maria must come to the Coach-door, as she wanted to speak to her, and that she must make haste and come immediately—"What an impertinent Message Mama!" said I—"Go Maria—" replied She—Accordingly I went and was obliged to stand there at her Ladyships pleasure though the Wind was extremely high and very cold. (*J* 201)

Austen liked this detail enough that she would reuse it in *Pride and Prejudice*, where Miss De Bourgh and Mrs. Jenkins stay in their phaeton at the gate and expect Charlotte to visit with them outside (*PP* II.5).

Not all of Austen's notations about manners in her letters and fictions emerge from the context of social inequality. In fact, letter-writing carries its own whole host of expectations about civility, fairness and interdependency, a code that seems to have caused Austen a certain amount of trouble in her own letter-writing life. Having to write a letter to someone you "owe" one to but for whom you don't feel a great deal of affection can provoke considerable discomfort (think about the feeling of sitting down to write a thank-you note to someone you don't much like for a present you didn't really want), and here Austen comments to her sister that she has received a letter of remonstrance from a mutual acquaintance for having failed to answer a letter:

> She supposes my silence may have proceeded from resentment of her not having written to inquire particularly after my hooping cough, &c. She is a funny one. I have answered her letter, and have endeavoured to give something like the truth with as little incivility as I could, by placing my silence to the want of subject in the very quiet way in which we live. (*JAL* 119)

Elsewhere it can be hard to disentangle the satirical element of Austen's observations about letter-writing from their underlying basis in fact: when their niece Fanny very suddenly gets married, without the appropriate permissions and notices, it precipitates a comic reflection on the tragedy of the fact that receiving a long letter is always more enjoyable than writing one: "I assure you I am as tired of writing long letters as you can be," Austen writes to Cassandra. "What a pity that one should still be so fond of receiving them!—Fanny Austen's Match is quite news, & I am sorry she has behaved so ill. There is some comfort to us in her misconduct, that we have not a congratulatory Letter to write" (*JAL* 143). That last sentence is a perfect example of what I would call "tongue-in-cheek" – it is a joke at her own and her sister's expense as well as an ironic comment on a situation that must have provoked genuine consternation and concern.

Another way of thinking about manners would be to say that we learn manners – we become mannerly – so as better to veil our own naked self-interest from ourselves and others. Bernard Mandeville's *Fable of the Bees* (1714) was demonized in eighteenth-century Britain for the cynical portrait it painted of how private vices (luxury) contributed to public benefits (prosperity), but a softened version of that interdependency stands behind the vision of Adam Smith's *Wealth of Nations* (1776) as well. In *An Enquiry into the Origin of Moral Virtue*, appended to the *Fable* in 1723, Mandeville provocatively makes the case for flattery as a necessary component of an education in virtue by considering "the Tricks made use of by the Women that would teach Children to be mannerly": a nurse praises a very young child for her curtsies, and her older sister

> wonders at the Perverseness of their Judgment, and swelling with Indignation, is ready to cry at the Injustice that is done her, till, being whisper'd in the Ear that it is only to please the Baby, and that she is a Woman, she grows proud at being let into the Secret, and rejoicing at the Superiority of her Understanding, repeats what has been said with large Additions, and insults over the Weakness of her Sister, whom all this while

she fancies to be the only Bubble among them. These extravagant Praises would by any one, above the Capacity of an Infant, be call'd fulsome Flatteries, and, if you will, abominable Lies, yet Experience teaches us, that by the help of such gross Encomiums, young Misses will be brought to make pretty Cur'sies, and behave themselves womanly much sooner, and with less trouble, than they would without them.[1]

The idea that flattery can lead to virtue has the paradoxical flavor that in our own time is often associated with the pop social-science of Malcolm Gladwell's *New Yorker* essays, the *Freakonomics* books and snappy titles like Steven Johnson's *Everything Bad Is Good For You: How Today's Popular Culture Is Actually Making Us Smarter*. The underlying logic of this sort of paradox is laid out especially well in one of the great works of twentieth-century intellectual history, A. O. Hirschman's *The Passions and the Interests*, which describes the desire of a wide range of eighteenth-century thinkers to develop a model of human motivation in which desire and self-interest could be productively yoked together to drive both individual and social goods.[2]

Austen is a subtle theorist of self-interest, with a keen eye for the ways it distorts behavior and affects people's explanations of the choices they make, and *Mansfield Park* contains an extended treatment of the ongoing balancing act between self-interest and other motives of sociability. It is Fanny Price's first real ball, a small party at Mansfield Park, and she is very keen to dance, but her desires are as usual disregarded by those around her. When Tom Bertram approaches Fanny, she hopes that he will invite her to join him on the floor, "but instead of asking her to dance, [he] drew a chair near her, and gave her an account of the present state of a sick horse, and the opinion of the groom, from whom he had just parted":

> Fanny found that it was not to be, and in the modesty of her nature immediately felt that she had been unreasonable in expecting it. When he had told of his horse, he took a newspaper from the table, and looking over it said in a languid way, "If you want to dance, Fanny, I will stand up with you."—With more than equal civility the offer was declined;–she did not wish to dance.—"I am glad of it," said he in a much brisker tone, and throwing down the newspaper again—"for I am tired to death. I only wonder how the good people can keep it up so long.—They had need be *all* in love, to find any amusement in such folly—and so they are, I fancy." (*MP* I.12, 139–40)

Tom hews to that Mandevillean belief that everything is motivated by self-interest, postulating that each person who is dancing is only doing it to gain physical and emotional proximity to an otherwise inaccessible love object, and his invitation to Fanny is merely cursory. Her own sensitivity to the needs of others (really it is a damaging hypersensitivity) in turn causes her to decline an offer that she believes not to align with Tom's own desires and interests.

Tom himself behaves exactly according to the Mandevillean imperatives he discerns in others, and is oblivious to the hypocrisy involved in castigating the self-interest of other people while roundly advancing his own preferences. When Mrs. Norris sees that Tom isn't dancing and asks him to join her table for cards, then, he readjusts his preferences in light of the new demand (there is a strongly game-theoretical flavor to Austen's treatment of this sequence of choices):[3]

> "I should be most happy," replied he aloud, and jumping up with alacrity, "it would give me the greatest pleasure—but that I am this moment going to dance. Come, Fanny,"—taking her hand—"do not be dawdling any longer, or the dance will be over."
>
> Fanny was led off very willingly, though it was impossible for her to feel much gratitude towards her cousin, or distinguish, as he certainly did, between the selfishness of another person and his own. (*MP* I.12, 140)

In case this judgment from Fanny by way of the narrator weren't clear enough, Austen shows us Tom complaining at length about the way Mrs. Norris has attempted to exert control over him even as he shows a complete lack of self-awareness that he has done exactly the same thing to Fanny, making use of her compliance to buttress his own wishes:

> "And to ask me in such a way too! Without ceremony, before them all, so as to leave me no possibility of refusing! *That* is what I dislike most particularly. It raises my spleen more than any thing, to have the pretence of being asked, of being given a choice, and at the same time addressed in such a way as to oblige one to do the very thing—whatever it be! If I had not luckily thought of standing up with you, I could not have got out of it. It is a great deal too bad. But when my aunt has got a fancy in her head, nothing can stop her." (*MP* I.12, 141)

In every novel of Austen's, the protagonist suffers from the bad manners of those around her. In *Pride and Prejudice*, those inflicting damage on Elizabeth Bennet are most of all her own family members. She is relatively impervious to the hurtfulness of the bad manners of those outside her family (Miss Bingley, Lady Catherine De Bourgh), but the discomfort of seeing her younger sisters, her mother and even (painfully) her father display their ill breeding in public is acute, and the novel suggests that we can suffer real costs as well as "mere" emotional pain and embarrassment on account of the behavior of those close to us. After an evening in which one family member after another has very publicly embarrassed him- or herself, the narrator observes: "To Elizabeth it appeared, that had her family made an agreement to expose themselves as much as they could during the evening, it would have been impossible for them to play their parts with more spirit, or finer success" (*PP* I.18, 114). It is these inadvertent revelations of profoundly bad manners that legitimately underlie Darcy's desire to separate Bingley from Jane: "There were some very strong objections against the lady," Colonel Fitzwilliam tells Elizabeth when she tries delicately to find out what really happened, wholly unaware that she has any personal investment in the business (*PP* II.10, 209). Elizabeth at that point in the novel is not ready to hear this, thinking indignantly of the virtues of her father and her older sister, but over the remainder of the novel it will emerge that Mr. Bennet's behavior has in certain respects been more profoundly culpable than his wife's, especially insofar as his better understanding and capabilities make his failures a matter of negligence rather than incompetence. Certainly both Elizabeth and Jane fear that Lydia's flagrantly bad behavior will cost the rest of the family a great deal (*PP* II.18, 256–57), a fear borne out by subsequent developments, though it is also Lydia's elopement that provides the means of bringing Elizabeth and Darcy together again.

I first read *Pride and Prejudice* when I was eight or nine, and I still believe that I understood most of it very well then, with two major exceptions. One was the dismissive treatment of Mary Bennet and her pretentions to intellectual distinction. As a bookish child, I did not see why the novel should be so critical of Mary's pronouncements and preferences, and it took reading other novels motivated by the concerns of the 1790s in my twenties (particularly novels such as Elizabeth Hamilton's *Memoirs of Modern Philosophers* (1800) and Amelia Opie's *Adeline Mowbray* (1804), both of which more directly take on arguments and tropes about women with intellectual aspirations who neglect the real virtues and ethical obligations of daughterhood or motherhood for quixotic programs of inappropriate reading) for me to understand that this character represents Austen's relatively late take on a well-worn critique of some of the more common distortions of female learning. The other thing I didn't fully understand, something that more profoundly limited my full comprehension of the book, was the harshness of the novel's ultimate verdict on Mr. Bennet.

Mr. Bennet is a likeable figure, for the most part; Elizabeth loves him dearly and wants to protect him against the judgment of others. But especially as we get to the end of the novel, the narrator shows us more clearly what the costs to his family have been, even beyond the failure to save money and protect his daughters' futures, of his laziness and negligence. "Had Elizabeth's opinions been all drawn from her own family, she could not have formed a very pleasing picture of conjugal felicity or domestic comfort," the chapter begins (*PP* II.19, 262). Mr. Bennet has reconciled himself to the consequence of his ill choice of a wife:

> Elizabeth, however, had never been blind to the impropriety of her father's behaviour as a husband. She had always seen it with pain; but respecting his abilities, and grateful for his affectionate treatment of herself, she endeavoured to forget what she could not overlook, and to banish from her thoughts that continual breach of conjugal obligation and decorum which, in exposing his wife to the contempt of her own children, was so highly reprehensible. (*PP* II.19, 262–63)

It is a strong judgment, and it is a necessary part of Elizabeth's awakening to true adulthood that she should be able to separate herself from a beloved but weak father to join in partnership with a man whose rectitude and strength of character turn out to have been unimpeachable even when she most disliked him.

This is not the only important dimension of Elizabeth's growth. At one point, when the Bennet sisters are commenting on Wickham's pursuit of the well-off Mary King, Lydia says that she is sure Wickham never really liked her for herself: "I will answer for it he never cared three straws about her," she pronounces. "Who *could* about such a nasty little freckled thing?" (*PP* II.16, 244). The narrator very clearly points out the change in Elizabeth that has occurred since she has begun to see the world in light of Mr. Darcy's knowledge of events and characters: "Elizabeth was shocked to think that, however incapable of such coarseness of *expression* herself, the coarseness of the *sentiment* was little other than her own breast had formerly harboured and fancied liberal!"

But if one strand of *Pride and Prejudice* involves ruthless judgment and discrimination (it is not a coincidence that the novel's happy ending involves the two most meritorious Bennet sisters moving far away from their parents), another strand of the novel rigorously critiques mistaken or ill-founded forms of discrimination, especially those based on birth rather than manners or behavior. This comes through most clearly, I think, in the final confrontation between Elizabeth and Lady Catherine. Lady

Catherine, having heard a rumor that Elizabeth is about to become engaged to her nephew, visits her at home to protest the notion of a cross-class alliance:

> "My daughter and my nephew are formed for each other. They are des-cended on the maternal side, from the same noble line; and, on the father's, from respectable, honourable, and ancient, though untitled families. Their fortune on both sides is splendid. They are destined for each other by the voice of every member of their respective houses; and what is to divide them? The upstart pretensions of a young woman without family, connections, or fortune. Is this to be endured! But it must not, shall not be. If you were sensible of your own good, you would not wish to quit the sphere, in which you have been brought up."
>
> "In marrying your nephew, I should not consider myself as quitting that sphere. He is a gentleman; I am a gentleman's daughter; so far we are equal."
>
> "True. You *are* a gentleman's daughter. But who was your mother? Who are your uncles and aunts? Do not imagine me ignorant of their condition."
> (*PP* III.14, 394–95)

Lady Catherine is giving voice to an older aristocratic position, while Elizabeth responds with a more modern updating of class distinction, but it is important that she too accepts the idea that there is such a thing as a "gentleman" and a genteel class. Very clear distinctions still operated in this period to divide the genteel from the working classes. Elizabeth is not altogether disavowing birth as a criterion of worth, but the novel rejects the notion that gentility is the preserve only of a tiny born elite; the marriage between Darcy and Elizabeth suggests the reinvigoration of the gentry-cum-aristocracy by way of marriage into robust middle-class stock, a marriage of equal merit and talents rather than a match based primarily on blood.

   In the context of what that marriage represents in terms of sociopolitical argument, Lady Catherine's rhetoric comes to sound hysterical and self-deluding, as when she tells Elizabeth that she is "no stranger to the particulars of [Lydia's] elopement" (of course, her own niece Georgiana Darcy very narrowly escaped a similar fate, though Lady Catherine doesn't know that):

> "I know it all; that the young man's marrying her, was a patched-up business, at the expence of your father and uncles. And is *such* a girl to be my nephew's sister? Is *her* husband, is the son of his late father's steward, to be his brother? Heaven and earth!—of what are you thinking? Are the shades of Pemberley to be thus polluted?" (*PP* III.14, 396)

Here, Lady Catherine's viewpoint is cast into doubt by her own hyperbole, and the third-person narration seems to endorse the reader's judgment against Lady Catherine's position: that term "polluted" is taken up playfully by the narrator in the book's second-to-last paragraph, in which Darcy's aunt has finally reconciled herself to the marriage and "condescended to wait on them at Pemberley, in spite of that pollution which its woods had received, not merely from the presence of such a mistress, but the visits of her uncle and aunt from the city" (*PP* III. 19, 430).[4]

In *Emma*, the use of arguments about manners to drive the story forward and precipitate social change is even more pronounced. This novel may contain Austen's most supreme comic instantiation of bad manners, the character of Mrs. Elton, whose name-dropping about her wealthy sister-in-law and the "barouche-landau" (she repeats the term three times over the course of a single paragraph – substitute something like "Bentley" or "Rolls-Royce" here and you will have a clearer sense of the effect) is only one of her annoying and vulgar habits. A good deal of awkwardness exists between Mrs. Elton and Emma on their first meeting, though it is a requirement of politeness that Emma, as first lady of the village, should pay Mrs. Elton a visit on her marriage (she has brought Harriet with her):

> The visit was of course short; and there was so much embarrassment and occupation of mind to shorten it, that Emma would not allow herself entirely to form an opinion of the lady, and on no account to give one, beyond the nothing-meaning terms of being "elegantly dressed, and very pleasing."
>
> She did not really like her. She would not be in a hurry to find fault, but she suspected that there was no elegance;—ease, but not elegance.—She was almost sure that for a young woman, a stranger, a bride, there was too much ease. Her person was rather good; her face not unpretty; but neither feature, nor air, nor voice, nor manner, were elegant. Emma thought at least it would turn out so.
>
> As for Mr. Elton, his manners did not appear—but no, she would not permit a hasty or a witty word from herself about his manners. It was an awkward ceremony at any time to be receiving wedding-visits, and a man had need be all grace to acquit himself well through it. The woman was better off; she might have the assistance of fine clothes, and the privilege of bashfulness, but the man had only his own good sense to depend on; and when she considered how peculiarly unlucky poor Mr. Elton was in being in the same room at once with the woman he had just married, the woman he had wanted to marry, and the woman whom he had been expected to marry, she must allow him to have the right to look as little wise, and to be as much affectedly, and as little really easy as could be. (*E* II.14, 291–92)

Ease of manner without elegance: you see how fine, how nuanced a set of terms is available to Austen for delineating social distinctions. The term "elegant" is reserved for someone genuinely a cut above the usual, and Mr. Elton's manners, though they are not actually given an adjective to describe them, clearly fall short of the standard of ease let alone of elegance. And yet there is also a hint here that Emma has made up her mind in advance of any actual evidence, and that her own judgments about manners and social class are more "interested" than she understands.

In his influential book *Distinction: A Cultural Critique of the Judgement of Taste*, French sociologist Pierre Bourdieu offers this formulation: "Taste classifies, and it classifies the classifier."[5] Mrs. Elton's continual breaches of taste, in the way she talks about people as well as things, will confirm Emma's initial sense that her manners are wanting. There are certain instabilities in Emma's own social position: she is the wealthiest and most socially elite woman of her circle, but as an unmarried woman she automatically has lower status than the genteel married women of her acquaintance. It's this discrepancy that licenses Mrs. Elton's frequent displays of condescension toward Emma, offering a way for Mrs. Elton to assert her own power in terms of their relative status. At one point, for instance, Mrs. Elton promises to introduce Emma to social life in Bath:

> It was as much as Emma could bear, without being impolite. The idea of her being indebted to Mrs. Elton for what was called an *introduction*—of her going into public under the auspices of a friend of Mrs. Elton's, probably some vulgar, dashing widow, who, with the help of a boarder, just made a shift to live!—The dignity of Miss Woodhouse, of Hartfield, was sunk indeed! (*E* II.14, 297)

These social solecisms of Mrs. Elton's, mostly issued with the design of puffing herself up and asserting her own high status, are enormously grating to Emma.

At one point Mrs. Elton shows her own bad manners by commenting on the surprisingly ladylike quality of Mrs. Weston's manners, an oblique reminder that Mrs. Weston formerly earned her living as a governess and a sideways dig at Emma that leaves Emma fuming; other breaches of manners include her inappropriately intimate use of "Knightley" (as opposed to the more proper "Mr. Knightley") as a form of address and her dreadful (it has something of the feel of "hubby" or "DH" in our own time) habit of calling her own husband "Mr. E." (*E* II.14, 300) and referring to him as her *caro sposo*. Most unpleasant of all, perhaps, are her patronizing ways toward Jane Fairfax. "Patronizing" is another of those words like "condescension" whose meaning was in transition during this period: patronage is still, circa 1800, a legitimate mode of advancement, and there are circumstances where you might want to be patronized (if you were a merchant who wanted someone's business) or desire patronage (if you were a young man who hoped to make a career in the church). But here, Mrs. Elton's attempts to serve as Jane's patroness meet with dislike even from Emma, who is hardly Jane's fondest advocate.

Mrs. Elton is vocal about having promised to find a "situation" (a post as governess) for Jane Fairfax, something that strikes Emma as utterly beyond the pale given Mrs. Elton's own lack, in her view, of any real claim to gentility or social influence. Here Emma is ranting after the fact to Mr. Knightley: "this is a punishment beyond what you can have merited!—The kindness and protection of Mrs. Elton!—'Jane Fairfax and Jane Fairfax.' Heavens! Let me not suppose that she dares go about, Emma Woodhouse-ing me!" (*E* II.15, 306). Properly Mrs. Elton should be referring to Jane as "Miss Fairfax," both to her face and when speaking about her to others – only very close friends and social equals would have referred to each other by their first names. Emma doesn't understand how Jane can tolerate this treatment, but Mr. Knightley offers a perceptive suggestion that makes more sense of it: "Mrs. Elton does not talk *to* Miss Fairfax as she speaks *of* her," he observes (*E* II.15, 309).

Hard-core advocates for sincerity, William Godwin prominent among them, thought that we *should* speak to people exactly as we speak about them behind their backs, but it would be hard to find many supporters for such an extreme position, and in the question of how we speak to people rather than of them, we come to the novel's moral crux, which falls during an important scene late in the excursion to Box Hill. Frank Churchill and Emma are joking with each other while everyone else is out of sorts, and Frank Churchill proposes a circle game. He asks from each person, on Emma's behalf, "either one thing very clever, be it prose or verse, original or repeated—or two things moderately clever—or three things very dull indeed, and she engages to laugh heartily at them all." The good-natured Miss Bates is willing to make a small joke at her own expense about this range of choices:

> "Oh! Very well," exclaimed Miss Bates, "then I need not be uneasy. 'Three things very dull indeed.' That will just do for me, you know. I shall be sure to say three dull things as soon as ever I open my mouth, shan't I?—(looking round with the most good-humoured dependence on every body's assent)— Do not you all think I shall?"
> Emma could not resist.

"Ah! ma'am, but there may be a difficulty. Pardon me—but you will be limited as to number—only three at once."

Miss Bates, deceived by the mock ceremony of her manner, did not immediately catch her meaning; but, when it burst on her, it could not anger, though a slight blush showed that it could pain her.

"Ah!—well—to be sure. Yes, I see what she means, (turning to Mr. Knightley,) and I will try to hold my tongue. I must make myself very disagreeable, or she would not have said such a thing to an old friend." (*E* III.7, 403)

I don't know to what extent we would condemn this moment ourselves, as readers, or find Emma deeply morally culpable for what is partly just an inability to resist showing off her own verbal ingenuity, but the novel stages a significant reproach for her in the form of Mr. Knightley's most severe reproof. He emphasizes the fact that Miss Bates is already vulnerable because of her poverty: "were she prosperous," he tells Emma,

"I could allow much for the occasional prevalence of the ridiculous over the good. Were she a woman of fortune, I would leave every harmless absurdity to take its chance, I would not quarrel with you for any liberties of manner. Were she your equal in situation—but, Emma, consider how far this is from being the case. She is poor; she has sunk from the comforts she was born to; and, if she live to old age, must probably sink more. Her situation should secure your compassion. It was badly done, indeed!" (*E* III.7, 408)

And the reproof, though Emma does not respond to Knightley directly, prompts a degree of self-reproach and self-revelation that is somewhat reminiscent of the experience of Elizabeth Bennet on reading and rereading Darcy's letter:

She was vexed beyond what could have been expressed—almost beyond what she could conceal. Never had she felt so agitated, mortified, grieved, at any circumstance in her life. She was most forcibly struck. The truth of his representation there was no denying. She felt it at her heart. How could she have been so brutal, so cruel to Miss Bates!—How could she have exposed herself to such ill opinion in any one she valued! And how suffer him to leave her without saying one word of gratitude, of concurrence, of common kindness! (*E* III.7, 409)

The skeptical reader may note that it is the fact of Mr. Knightley's thinking badly of her, rather than deep remorse about the cruelty of her words to Miss Bates, that seems to be emphasized by the language here, and many readers have felt about *Emma* that the novel's drama of correction and submission is undermined or at least ironized by the fact that Emma is the stronger personality of the two and has no good reason to reform herself permanently. I think this ambivalence or uncertainty is embedded in the novel's very language; at the very least, it's something that can be argued back and forth nearly endlessly.

What else had Emma to wish for, asks the narrator, following her engagement to Mr. Knightley, then answers the question: "What had she to wish for? Nothing, but to grow more worthy of him, whose intentions and judgment had been ever so superior to her own. Nothing, but that the lessons of her past folly might teach her humility and circumspection in future" (*E* III.18, 518–19). Is Emma actually going to learn "humility and circumspection," though? Is that realistic? (Remember, too, the very funny passage earlier on in which Emma, ashamed at the emotional pain her mistakes have caused Harriet, has "every previous resolution confirmed of being humble and discreet, and repressing imagination all the rest of her life" (I.17, 153).) The exaggerated language may give us reason to suspect that Emma is experiencing only a fleeting moment of self-correction, and that though we can work hard to modify our habits and behavior, our underlying inclinations and affinities may be harder to repress over the long term.

CHAPTER 5

Morals

One of the clearest moral positions taken in Austen's novels involves the critique of overly harsh forms of morality that call themselves Christian but that bear little resemblance to the values of the New Testament. The novels are in important respects committed to Christian values, but without being rigid or doctrinaire, and they regularly temper judgment with humility. Jane and Elizabeth Bennet suffer deep distress as a consequence of their sister Lydia's lack of regard for the prohibition on sex before marriage (it is a Christian prohibition as well as a powerful conventional expectation of women in this period), but their joint response to her transgression is humane, emphasizing the hope of reclamation. In contrast, several other characters who more strongly self-identify as Christian moralists come down with laughable severity on Lydia's offense. This is Mary Bennet's judgment on Lydia's elopement:

> "Unhappy as the event must be for Lydia, we may draw from it this useful lesson; that loss of virtue in a female is irretrievable—that one false step involves her in endless ruin—that her reputation is no less brittle than it is beautiful,—and that she cannot be too much guarded in her behaviour towards the undeserving of the other sex." (*PP* III.5, 319)

Her uttering of these conventional platitudes about women's chastity doesn't give them any credibility, it just shows their hollowness, not to mention the ill fit between such rigid prohibitions and the very real temptations of life in the world for a girl who, we might remember, is only sixteen years old when she runs off with Wickham.

Once Wickham has married Lydia, the couple regains some social countenance, an important part of reclaiming them for the norms and values endorsed by the society at large. Mr. Bennet initially states that he won't receive the newly married couple at Longbourn, on the ground that socially sanctioning the outcome of improper behavior would encourage the young couple's "impudence" (*PP* III.8, 342), but Elizabeth and Jane are able to persuade him that the entire family will benefit by putting unpleasant rumors to rest by way of an official visit home (*PP* III.8, 346). In the moral framework of Austen's novels, concern for the proprieties – for reputation, broadly conceived – is not the mark of shallowness but rather an appropriate acknowledgment of the obligations of sociability, with ethics and etiquette deeply intertwined.

The novel presents one other flourish on Mr. Bennet's handling of the marriage. It is a comical indictment of Mrs. Bennet's failure to understand the deeper principles of matrimony:

> Mrs. Bennet found, with amazement and horror, that her husband would not advance a guinea to buy clothes for his daughter. He protested that she should receive from him no mark of affection whatever, on the occasion. Mrs. Bennet could hardly comprehend it. That his anger could be carried to such a point of inconceivable resentment, as to refuse his daughter a privilege, without which her marriage would scarcely seem valid, exceeded all that she could believe possible. She was more alive to the disgrace, which the want of new clothes must reflect on her daughter's nuptials, than to any sense of shame at her eloping and living with Wickham, a fortnight before they took place. (*PP* III.8, 343)

Mrs. Bennet's shallowness is mocked in this passage, but the novel reserves a more profound indictment for strict exertions of conventional moral judgment that aren't tempered by the humility and humanity – the empathy, we might call it – that should properly accompany verdicts on other people's wrongdoing. Austen herself, in her letters as in her fiction, would probably have phrased this point in more explicitly Christian terms, invoking forgiveness rather than sympathy or empathy and resolutely condemning the hypocrisy and mean-spiritedness of Christians unwilling to comprehend and forgive transgression.

Mr. Collins' letter to Mr. Bennet in the wake of Lydia's elopement provides the novel's most extreme instance of such a judgment:

> I am truly rejoiced that my cousin Lydia's sad business has been so well hushed up, and am only concerned that their living together before the marriage took place, should be so generally known. I must not, however, neglect the duties of my station, or refrain from declaring my amazement, at hearing that you received the young couple into your house as soon as they were married. It was an encouragement of vice; and had I been the rector of Longbourn, I should very strenuously have opposed it. You ought certainly to forgive them as a christian, but never to admit them in your sight, or allow their names to be mentioned in your hearing. (*PP* III.15, 403)

"*That* is his notion of Christian forgiveness!" Mr. Bennet aptly comments; but the novel also clearly critiques Mr. Collins' disproportionate attention to the widespread knowledge of the transgression rather than to the transgression itself. It is not presumptuous for a clergyman to think that it is an important part of his job to discourage vice; think for instance of Edmund, in *Mansfield Park*, arguing that clergymen must influence public manners, albeit not as "arbiters of good breeding": "The *manners* I speak of, might rather be called *conduct*, perhaps, the result of good principles; the effect, in short, of those doctrines which it is their duty to teach and recommend" (*MP* I.9, 109). But Mr. Collins' understanding of good conduct and good principles is seen to be sorely lacking.

It was a commonplace, among the Mr. Collinses of the world, that novels were one of the most pernicious influences on contemporary morality, most especially on the morals of female readers. Over Austen's career as a writer, she developed a number of arguments about the relationship between novel-reading and morality that worked overwhelmingly to counter what she saw as an ill-founded presumption that novels could only influence readers in negative ways. Certainly she was ready, especially in her earlier writings, to mock some of the values encapsulated in the sentimental novel after the fashion of Jean-Jacques Rousseau's *Julie, ou la Nouvelle Héloïse* (1761). The heroines of "Love and Freindship," a short novel that includes inset letters, have names that signal their "novelistic" identities – Laura, Marianne, Sophia – and ardently and foolishly aver the antiestablishment values of sentimental fiction. Laura is highly critical, for instance, of a young woman visitor who fails to live up to those values: "She staid by half an hour and neither in the Course of her Visit, confided to me any of her Secret thoughts, nor requested me to confide in her, any of Mine. You will easily imagine therefore my Dear Marianne that I could not feel any ardent Affection or very sincere Attachment for Lady Dorothea" (*J* 112). This is silly but funny, and only represents a slight exaggeration of the position you might have found a real novel heroine propounding in this period.

It is not just the letter-writers of "Love and Freindship" but its narrator as well who endorses a sentimental discourse that Austen depicts as selfishly heedless of familial and social obligation: "After having so nobly disentangled themselves from the Shackles of Parental Authority, by a Clandestine Marriage," states the narrator of the story's pair of heroines, "they were determined never to forfeit the good opinion they had gained in the World, in so doing, by accepting any proposals of reconciliation that might be offered them by their Fathers—to this farther trial of their noble independence however they were never exposed" (*J* 116). I might add here that we have no evidence that Austen questioned parental authority in her own life, though she had an easier relationship with her father than with her mother and the years following her father's death were painful ones, not least because of the implicit expectation – indeed, the necessity – that brothers should take on the mantle of familial governance over their unmarried sisters. The story's underlying criticism of the rhetoric of noble emancipation from parental shackles is clear, and is stated even more explicitly elsewhere in the tale; when Augustus and Sophia, who have eloped with the help of money stolen from his father, run out of money, the narrator says, "they, Exalted Creatures!, scorned to reflect a moment on their pecuniary Distresses and would have blushed at the idea of paying their Debts" (*J* 116).

The world is not so sympathetic to their values as the narrator, though, and to Laura's chagrin, Augustus is arrested and their possessions are taken away by creditors. "Ah! What could we do but what we did!" Laura comments philosophically. "We sighed and fainted on the Sofa" (*J* 117). It is a fine verdict on the salience of sentimental values to real-life calamity. And of course there are Sophia's dying words to Laura, more a mockery of the trappings of sentimentality than an indictment of sentimental morality as such, but certainly making the point that sentimentalism justifies an ideology of self, even of selfishness enlisted in the aid of self-destruction, that no rational sociable person could sanction:

> "My beloved Laura (said she to me a few Hours before she died) take warning from my unhappy End and avoid the imprudent conduct which has occasioned it . . . Beware of fainting-fits . . . Though at the time they may be refreshing and Agreable yet believe me they will in the end, if too often repeated and at improper seasons, prove destructive to your Constitution . . . My fate will teach you this . . . I die a Martyr to my greif for the loss of Augustus . . . One fatal swoon has cost me my Life . . . Beware of swoons Dear Laura . . . A frenzy fit is not one quarter so pernicious; it is an exercise to the Body and if not too violent, is I dare say conductive to Health in its consequences—Run mad as often as you chuse; but do not faint—."
> (*J* 132–33)

The playful indictment of sentimentality that we see all over Austen's juvenilia finds a more serious counterpart in the novel she left unfinished at her death. *Sanditon* is explicitly satirical in ways that recall the early works, including *Northanger Abbey*, not least when it voices a critique of a young man called Sir Edward Denham, a lover of novels (these are his own words, and he condemns himself out of his own mouth even as Austen relishes the parody) in which "the strong spark of woman's captivations elicit such fire in the soul of man as leads him—(though at the risk of some aberration from the strict line of primitive obligations)—to hazard all, dare all, achieve all, to obtain her.—Such are the works which I peruse with delight, and I hope I may say, with amelioration" (*LM* 182). The high-flown jargon Sir Edward prefers does little to mask the fact that his preference is for novels in which men pursue women for their own sexual satisfaction, possibly at the cost of actual rape, and it can be at best disingenuous and at worst dangerously misguided to believe that reading this kind of book makes one a better person. The narrator sums up harshly:

> The truth was that Sir Edward, whom circumstances had confined very much to one spot, had read more sentimental novels than agreed with him. His fancy had been early caught by all the impassioned and most exceptionable parts of Richardson's; and such authors as have since appeared to treat in Richardson's steps, so far as man's determined pursuit of woman in defiance of every opposition of feeling and convenience is concerned, had since occupied the greater part of his literary hours, and formed his character.—With a perversity of judgement, which must be attributed to his not having by nature a very strong head, the graces, the spirit, the ingenuity, and the perseverance, of the villain of the story outweighed all his absurdities and all his atrocities with Sir Edward. With him, such conduct was genius, fire and feeling.—It interested and inflamed him; and he was always more anxious for its success and mourned over its discomfitures with more tenderness than could ever have been contemplated by the authors. (*LM* 183)

Austen admired Richardson greatly, and this passage makes quite clear that Sir Edward is misreading a novel like *Clarissa*, or at least reading it very selectively – and yet such novels do contain the germs of an ideology of seduction and domination.

The satire on novels in *Northanger Abbey* may be the place where Austen makes her clearest and most explicit defense of fiction as a way of improving morality, an agent of genuine amelioration. Young Catherine Morland prefers outdoor activities to books, at least if they are "books of information":

> for, provided that nothing like useful knowledge could be gained from them, provided they were all story and no reflection, she had never any objection to books at all. But from fifteen to seventeen she was in training of a heroine; she read all such works as heroines must read to supply their memories with those quotations which are so serviceable and so soothing in the vicissitudes of their eventful lives. (*NA* I.1, 7)

The tone of the satire here is affectionate rather than damning, and it is followed not much later by what is probably the most famous defense of novel-reading in all of Austen's fiction. Catherine's intimate friendship with Isabella has proceeded apace, to the point that when the weather is bad, they "shut themselves up, to read novels together":

> Yes, novels;–for I will not adopt that ungenerous and impolitic custom so common with novel writers, of degrading by their contemptuous censure the very performances, to the number of which they are themselves adding— joining with their greatest enemies in bestowing the harshest epithets on such works, and scarcely ever permitting them to be read by their own heroine, who if she accidentally take up a novel, is sure to turn over its insipid pages with disgust. Alas! If the heroine of one novel be not patronized by the heroine of another, from whom can she expect protection and regard? I cannot approve of it. (*NA* I.5, 30)

The narrator goes on to regret the fact that so many speak lightly or even disrespectfully of novels: why should a young lady, asked what she is reading, say that it is "only" a novel? "'It is only Cecilia, or Camilla, or Belinda;' or, in short, only some work in which the greatest powers of the mind are displayed, in which the most thorough knowledge of human nature, the happiest delineation of its varieties, the liveliest effusions of wit and humour are conveyed to the world in the best chosen language" (*NA* I.5, 31).

The first two novels named here are by Frances Burney, probably Austen's single most direct model, while the third is written by Maria Edgeworth (and has a heroine strongly reminiscent of Elinor Dashwood); all three can be described as realistic fiction, novels of manners and morals that influenced Austen a great deal ("I have made up my mind to like no Novels really, but Miss Edgeworth's, Yours & my own," Austen wrote to the niece whose novel draft she was reading (*JAL* 289)). And *Northanger Abbey* also takes the trouble to note that novel-reading is suitable for more than just women: Henry Tilney, well-informed as he is, is also a great novel-reader. Catherine has naïvely imagined that novels are not "clever enough" for him ("gentlemen read better books," she says), but "The person, be it gentleman or lady, who has not pleasure in a good novel," Henry tells her in response, "must be intolerably stupid" (*NA* I.14, 107).

Reading has an impact not just on the intellect but on the character, and while novels offer knowledge of human nature, true morality must also be a matter of Christianity, with Austen's ethics always strongly grounded (to a degree modern secular readers may be uncomfortable acknowledging) in religious belief and observance. The intellect should of course be built up by way of information and understanding, and this will involve reading history and essays along the lines of the course of reading Fanny Price undertakes with her younger sister Susan in the third volume of *Mansfield Park*. It is perhaps poetry rather than the novel that offers the greater danger to readers of sensibility: the cultivation of sensibility past a certain point can be damaging both to the individual reader and to the society at large. The argument against reading too much poetry – or reading it too immersively – is summed up most clearly during Anne Elliot's conversation with the recently bereaved Captain Benwick about their shared love of poetry:

> he shewed himself so intimately acquainted with all the tenderest songs of the one poet [Scott], and all the impassioned descriptions of hopeless agony of the other [Byron]; he repeated, with such tremulous feeling, the various lines which imaged a broken heart, or a mind destroyed by wretchedness, and looked so entirely as if he meant to be understood, that she ventured to hope he did not always read only poetry; and to say, that she thought it was the misfortune of poetry, to be seldom safely enjoyed by those who enjoyed it completely; and that the strong feelings which alone could estimate it truly, were the very feelings which ought to taste it but sparingly. (*P* I.11, 108)

We can learn a good deal about Austen's own values, I think, from the advice Anne goes on to give to the young captain: "she ventured to recommend a larger allowance of prose in his daily study ... such works of our best moralists, such collections of the finest letters, such memoirs of characters of worth and suffering, as occurred to her at the moment as calculated to rouse and fortify the mind by the highest precepts, and the strongest examples of moral and religious endurances" (*P* I.11, 109) – and in case Anne sounds offputtingly pious or overly moral here, we are told not long after that she is afraid "that, like many other great moralists and preachers, she had been eloquent on a point in which her own conduct would ill bear examination" (*P* I.11, 109).

The two novels of Austen's that most clearly and explicitly stage arguments about different systems of manners and morals are *Sense and Sensibility* and *Mansfield Park*, and the last part of this chapter will offer fuller discussion of those two books. Elinor and Marianne Dashwood are immensely dear to one another, but they espouse distinctly different systems of values, a contrast that is drawn out early in the novel during an affectionate confrontation between the two sisters. Marianne, Elinor says teasingly, has "already ascertained Mr. Willoughby's opinion in almost every matter of importance" (*SS* I.10, 57): she and Willoughby both assent to all of the touchstones for romantic sensibility, including a love for the poetry of Cowper and Scott, a preference for ruined picturesque beauty over pastoral prosperity and a belief that second marriages are immoral (immortal love for the original spouse should render any subsequent attachment akin to bigamy).

Marianne doesn't take her sister's teasing in particularly good humor. In her passionate rejoinder, she caricatures Elinor's position in order to dismiss it outright: "I have been too much at my ease, too happy, too frank. I have erred against every common-place notion of decorum; I have been open and sincere where I ought to have been reserved, spiritless, dull, and deceitful:—had I talked only of the weather and the roads, and had I spoken only once in ten minutes, this reproach would have been spared." As Marianne frames the clash of values, indeed, Elinor represents mere manners (convention, decorum) while Marianne holds the high ground of morality; in this view, only the most outspoken, passionate and sincere forms of self-expression are legitimate (these are the values of Rousseau and of the forms of romanticism that followed in his wake, including literary exemplars like Goethe's immensely popular and influential novel *The Sorrows of Young Werther* (1774)), while the forms of politeness to which Elinor adheres can be thought of as institutionalized forms of hypocrisy, and therefore despised and dismissed.

The imperatives of sincerity and politeness can be difficult to balance in any given context, but tension between the two had a large-scale hot-button topicality in the 1790s, when revolutionary values especially hewed to sincerity. *Sense and Sensibility* was initially drafted during this decade, pretty certainly as an epistolary novel, and though it was significantly rewritten later on, it bears strong traces of those 1790s preoccupations.[1] Elinor's argument, considered on its own terms rather than in Marianne's unkind paraphrase, doesn't just have to do with the ways politeness protects others against our own aggression; it centers on the ways that politeness, as it bleeds into qualities such as self-control and self-command, is crucial for protecting our own vulnerable selves from the ravages of painful emotion. Marianne throws herself headlong into the relationship with Willoughby in a way that will open her up to immensely costly and damaging emotional consequences, not just to social embarrassment. Here is the narrator's summing-up of their respective positions:

> Elinor could not be surprised at their attachment. She only wished that it were less openly shewn; and once or twice did venture to suggest the

propriety of some self-command to Marianne. But Marianne abhorred all
concealment where no real disgrace could attend unreserve; and to aim at
the restraint of sentiments which were not in themselves illaudable,
appeared to her not merely an unnecessary effort, but a disgraceful subjec-
tion of reason to common-place and mistaken notions. (*SS* I.11, 63–64)

Pride comes before a fall, and the novel pretty clearly shows the costs of
Marianne's point of view.

Marianne is brought over to Elinor's position by the end of the book, and
there are other ways in which the novel strongly supports Elinor's perspective
against her sister's. Think of the elegantly constructed moment when Elinor
asserts that wealth is important for happiness and Marianne counters with the
proposition that money is not important once one is in possession of what she
calls "a competence" (*SS* I.17, 105). Elinor is skeptical, charging that "*Your*
competence and *my* wealth are very much alike, I dare say"; it emerges that
Marianne has in mind, as a modest competence, an annual income of eighteen
hundred or two thousand pounds, while Elinor's definition of wealth is only
half that. When Marianne realizes that Elinor has known for four months
about Edward's engagement to Lucy, she is staggered, but it offers Elinor an
opportunity to articulate an important moral lesson: she has been calm and
cheerful, she says, because she felt that she was doing her duty, not least
because "I owed it to my family and friends, not to create in them a solicitude
about me, which it could not be in my power to satisfy" (*SS* III.1, 297).
Marianne responds by imagining that Elinor's self-command comes easily to
her, a misconstrual that prompts an outburst in which Elinor is finally able to
express her feelings fully:

> "It was told me,—it was in a manner forced on me by the very person
> herself, whose prior engagement ruined all my prospects; and told me, as
> I thought, with triumph . . . If you can think me capable of ever feeling—
> surely you may suppose that I have suffered *now*. The composure of mind
> with which I have brought myself at present to consider the matter, the
> consolation that I have been willing to admit, have been the effect of
> constant and painful exertion;–they did not spring up of themselves;–they
> did not occur to relieve my spirits at first—No, Marianne.—*Then*, if I had
> not been bound to silence, perhaps nothing could have kept me entirely—
> not even what I owed to my dearest friends—from openly shewing that
> I was *very* unhappy." (*SS* III.1, 299–300)

Yet even as the novel contrasts Elinor's prudential, deeply self-protective
commitment to convention and moderation with Marianne's passionate
adherence to sincerity, it also postulates that the Dashwood sisters have
a great deal in common, especially when considered beside all of the novel's

other exemplars of bad manners: the cold, selfish Mrs. John Dashwood, the vulgar, self-promoting Lucy Steele, the disorders of feeling and taste personified in Lady Middleton and her sister Mrs. Palmer. Elinor is far from being a shallow person of convention. She honors a promise, for instance, even when it is made to someone she despises: her rectitude regarding the promise to Lucy Steele not to reveal anything about the secret engagement is striking, and she is also horrified when she hears a story from Miss Steele about Lucy and Edward that has been learned via eavesdropping.

> "How!" cried Elinor; "have you been repeating to me what you only learnt yourself by listening at the door? I am sorry I did not know it before; for I certainly would not have suffered you to give me particulars of a conversation which you ought not to have known yourself. How could you behave so unfairly by your sister?"
> "Oh, la! there is nothing in *that*. I only stood at the door, and heard what I could. And I am sure Lucy would have done just the same by me; for a year or two back, when Martha Sharpe and I had so many secrets together, she never made any bones of hiding in a closet, or behind a chimney-board, on purpose to hear what we said." (*SS* III.2, 311)

Marianne and Elinor are more similar than different not just because they both suffer painfully from loving men who disappoint them. They also share a set of values that would condemn the systems of thought featured in selfish characters' beliefs and behaviors.

Elinor has a good deal of sympathy for Willoughby, in spite of how much pain he has caused her sister. The scene in which Willoughby turns up late at night at the house where Marianne is lying desperately ill reads almost like a gothic eruption of melodrama into a novel that is otherwise firmly in the realistic mode of a novel of manners: "The night was cold and stormy," begins the narrator (*SS* III.7, 357), and a romantic intensity colors Willoughby's appearance at what he believes may be Marianne's deathbed to plead his case to Elinor. This is Elinor's analysis, after she has heard Willoughby's story:

> Her thoughts were silently fixed on the irreparable injury which too early an independence and its consequent habits of idleness, dissipation, and luxury, had made in the mind, the character, the happiness, of a man who, to every advantage of person and talents, united a disposition naturally open and honest, and a feeling, affectionate temper . . . Each faulty propensity in leading him to evil, had led him likewise to punishment. (*SS* III.8, 375)

She is swayed, she understands, by "circumstances which ought not in reason to have weight; by that person of uncommon attraction, that open, affectionate, and lively manner which it was no merit to possess; and by that still ardent love for Marianne, which it was not even innocent to indulge. But she felt that it was so, long, long before she could feel his influence less" (*SS* III.9, 377). And indeed, when she shares his story with Marianne, she doesn't want to "rouse such feelings in another, by her retailed explanation, as had at first been called forth in herself. Reflection had given calmness to her judgment, and sobered her own opinion of Willoughby's deserts;–she wished, therefore, to declare only the simple truth, and lay open such facts as were really due to his character, without any embellishment of tenderness to lead the fancy astray" (*SS* III.11, 395).

Elinor's verdict is that "all Willoughby's difficulties have arisen from the first offence against virtue, in his behavior to Eliza Williams. That crime has been the origin of every lesser one, and of all his present discontents" (*SS* III.11, 399). We always have to be careful about distinguishing between the position a narrator takes, the argument a novel develops as a whole (in which a plot outcome might, for instance, be at odds with arguments persuasively articulated by individual characters) and the beliefs of the real historical author, but we have no reason in this case to dispute the idea that Austen roundly backs her protagonist's conclusion. It might be added that the "offence against virtue" isn't defined as such merely because it involves sex outside marriage. It also centers on a privileged young man taking advantage of a woman intellectually weaker and more socially vulnerable than he is, and on his failure to assure that the consequences for her are tolerable, even in the most practical sense.

Marianne is ultimately brought over to Elinor's position on the importance of the proprieties. She has had a chance during her illness to reflect on the imperatives of self-command and of consideration for the self and others, and thought and experience have radically changed her understanding of the earlier relationship with Willoughby:

> "I considered the past; I saw in my own behaviour since the beginning of our acquaintance with him last autumn, nothing but a series of imprudence towards myself, and want of kindness to others. I saw that my own feelings had prepared my sufferings, and that my want of fortitude under them had almost led me to the grave. My illness, I well know, had been entirely brought on by myself by such negligence of my own health, as I had felt even at the time to be wrong. Had I died,—it would have been self-destruction. I did not know my danger till the danger was removed; but with such feelings as these reflections gave me, I wonder at my recovery,—wonder that the very eagerness of my desire to live, to have time for atonement to my God, and to you all, did not kill me at once." (*SS* III.10, 391)

Religious doctrine prohibits suicide, and this is part of why Marianne understands her own behavior to have been wrong, but it would be too narrow to think of this as "merely" a religious prohibition; it is grounded, rather, in a broad and deep ethical argument about care for oneself and others (think, for instance, of the resolutely secular arguments against suicide writer Jennifer Michael Hecht has made in her book *Stay: A History of Suicide and the Philosophies Against It*).

In the end, though these arguments about morality are strongly articulated and prosecuted, the book also shades them with humor and irony. Marianne's reversal of opinion is summed up by the narrator with affectionate satire:

> Marianne Dashwood was born to an extraordinary fate. She was born to discover the falsehood of her own opinions, and to counteract, by her conduct, her most favourite maxims. She was born to overcome an affection formed so late in life as seventeen, and with no sentiment superior to strong esteem and lively friendship, voluntarily to give her hand to another!—and *that* other, a man who had suffered no less than herself under the event of a former attachment, whom, two years before, she had considered too old to be married,—and who still sought the constitutional safe-guard of a flannel waistcoat! (*SS* III.14, 429)

Austen the novelist is also concerned to make sure that we don't think of this as a crude morality tale in which the good must be rewarded and the bad punished; the novel displays a debunking impulse that undermines or at least somewhat complicates its own moral certainties. Willoughby repents his cruelty to Marianne, but he is not "for ever inconsolable" (*SS* III.14, 430): he leads a perfectly happy life, with horses, dogs and hunting providing "no inconsiderable degree of domestic felicity." The language lightly ironizes this fate, but I think we are meant to take seriously the notion that life goes on, and to understand that most people will mix good and bad in their behavior, with fortune not always running in strict proportion to what a moralist might consider just deserts.

Mansfield Park probably offers Austen's deepest treatment of the relationship between morals and manners. The novel constructs an extended argument for the importance of maintaining a religious and ethical life, with those of good character certainly taking into account questions of propriety but most importantly resisting undue pressure from those whose power and wealth gives them authority over us. Readers have not always agreed on what the novel's argument actually is, of course, and I will pause periodically in my analysis to think about the ways in which Austen's stated argument seems to be complicated or even actively undercut by evidence elsewhere in the novel. One strand of *Mansfield Park*'s moral argument concerns the importance of making sure that children's education depends on underlying principles that are ethical and religious rather than chiefly worldly, principles of self-sacrifice and service to others rather than self-ishness and social distinction. Mrs. Norris is in many respects the book's worst villain, while Sir Thomas comes across as an exemplar of patriarchal values and cares who reveals the damaging weaknesses that may accompany that kind of governance rather than displaying an idealized version of its strengths.

Edward Said makes *Mansfield Park* a central piece of evidence in the case he builds, in *Culture and Imperialism*, about literature becoming a battleground for politics and ideology in the age of imperialism, with one of the key powers of narration being the choice of which stories to tell: "precisely because Austen is so summary in one context, so provocatively rich in the other," he writes, alluding to the presence-in-absence of the story of the Bertram property in Antigua, "precisely because of that imbalance we are able to move in on the novel, reveal and accentuate the interdependence scarcely mentioned on its brilliant pages."[2] Playwright and political activist Harold Pinter's performance of the role of Sir Thomas forms one of the most memorable aspects of Patricia Rozema's 1999 film adaptation of *Mansfield Park*, and that film itself provides an unusually explicit instance of a literary-critical argument directly informing an ima-ginative adaptation of a novel in another medium.

The intellectual blind spot of the aristocratic position comes through in Sir Thomas' early words of warning about the consequences of bringing the poor dependent cousin Fanny Price into the Bertram household:

> "There will be some difficulty in our way, Mrs. Norris, as to the distinction proper to be made between the girls as they grow up; how to preserve in the minds of my *daughters* the consciousness of what they are, without making them think too lowly of their cousin; and how, without depressing her spirits too far, to make her remember that she is not a *Miss Bertram*. I should wish to see them very good friends, and would, on no account, authorize in my girls the smallest degree of arrogance towards their relation; but still they cannot be equals. Their rank, fortune, rights, and expectations, will always be different. It is a point of great delicacy, and you must assist us in our endeavours to choose exactly the right line of conduct." (*MP* I.1, 11–12)

I suppose that there is nothing wrong with these words, on the face of things: fortune and expectations are inextricably tied in this world. But are "rights" different for young women raised under the same familial roof in the same way that rank and fortune might be, and should social stature make as much difference as Sir Thomas thinks? The fatal flaw built into Sir Thomas' vision of distinction is compounded by the poor choices made by Aunt Norris, who rewards the sisters for superficial achievements and fails to encourage them to be kind, self-sacrificing and charitable. Edmund Bertram is imbued with all of those qualities, by the way, but the novel seems to emphasize the ways in which women especially are expected to learn to be good not just by giving but by giving things up, a morality of self-sacrifice that the novel simultaneously celebrates and calls into question.

Mansfield Park taps into an existing conversation about what were often just called "female accomplishments" – young women learning to play the piano, embroider, paint and so forth – and joins a larger chorus of voices leveled against fashionable accomplishments coming at the expense of other kinds of learning (Edgeworth's novel *Patronage*, published the same year as *Mansfield Park*, offers an uncannily close analogue). The Bertram sisters are highly accomplished and not at all self-conscious about displaying their talents as a matter of distinction, and there is often no adult present to remind them that this sort of superficial polish and self-display is hardly the be-all and end-all of education; their mother is borderline negligent, and Sir Thomas seems not to be involved with the day-to-day minutiae of their upbringing even before he leaves for Antigua. When they gloat, after Fanny first comes, about how much they know and how little she does, Aunt Norris merely tells them to "remember that, if you are ever so forward and clever yourselves, you should always be modest; for, much as you know already, there is a great deal more for you to learn" (*MP* I.2, 21). Showing that she has understood the real unspoken spirit of Mrs. Norris' point, the unnamed Bertram daughter simply responds: "Yes, I know there is, till I am seventeen."

In case these words do not sufficiently condemn the girl, the narrator offers a tart further summing-up of what's wrong with this manner of education: "Such were the counsels by which Mrs. Norris assisted to form her nieces' minds; and it is not very wonderful that with all their promising talents and early information, they should be entirely deficient in the less common acquirements of self-knowledge, generosity, and humility" (*MP* I.2, 21–22). The indictment of the Bertram girls' shallowness – and of the failure of education their behavior represents – continues throughout this early section of the novel, as when the narrator notes their popularity in the neighborhood at large: "Their vanity was in such good order, that they seemed to be quite free from it, and gave themselves no airs; while the praises attending such behaviour, secured, and brought round by their

aunt, served to strengthen them in believing they had no faults" (*MP*
I.4, 40).

The Crawford siblings' arrival profoundly disrupts Mansfield's equili-
brium, with the possibility for change having been opened up especially by
the patriarch's departure for his colonial property in Antigua. Henry
Crawford, a charismatic and attractive man, interests both of the
Bertram sisters, including the one who is already engaged to someone
else, and he displays a true mix of good and bad qualities. He will find his
own version of selfish enjoyment not in overeating like his brother-in-law
Dr. Grant or in over-frugality after the fashion of Mrs. Norris but in
working to make the Bertram sisters like him more than is proper: "He
did not want them to die of love," the narrator comments; "but with sense
and temper which ought to have made him judge and feel better, he
allowed himself great latitude on such points" (*MP* I.5, 52). It is not very
creditable on the Miss Bertrams' part that they give in so readily to his
flirtations. When he goes away for two weeks, it is

> a fortnight of such dullness to the Miss Bertrams, as ought to have put them
> both on their guard, and made even Julia admit in her jealousy of her sister,
> the absolute necessity of distrusting his attentions, and wishing him not to
> return; and a fortnight of sufficient leisure in the intervals of shooting and
> sleeping, to have convinced the gentleman that he ought to keep longer
> away, had he been more in the habit of examining his own motives, and of
> reflecting to what the indulgence of his idle vanity was tending; but,
> thoughtless and selfish from prosperity and bad example, he would not
> look beyond the present moment. (*MP* I.12, 135)

What we learn here is that for self-protective reasons alone (shades,
perhaps, of Elinor and Marianne Dashwood), Julia Bertram should have
examined her own feelings more closely and thought about the dangers
Henry's friendship poses to her sister and herself; and that Henry Crawford
is even more culpable than the two girls. His vanity is "idle" rather than
malicious, he's not a wanton seducer and abuser, but the "tendency" of his
behavior goes all in one direction, one that is profoundly immoral not just
because it will culminate in an episode of adulterous sex but because it fails
to grant other people the proper autonomy and consideration that are the
foundations of right society.

The novel develops in a number of different ways a central assertion
concerning the importance of thoughtfulness of others, including emphasizing the willingness to give up one's own pleasures and satisfactions
because they conflict with the needs and desires of another person.
We are told, for instance, of Julia's discomfort when she is trapped

listening to Mrs. Rushworth at a time when she wants desperately to be walking in the park with Henry Crawford: "The politeness which she had been brought up to practice as a duty, made it impossible for her to escape; while the want of that higher species of self-command, that just consideration of others, that knowledge of her own heart, that principle of right which had not formed any essential part of her education, made her miserable under it" (*MP* I.9, 106). It's not just that Julia doesn't experience satisfaction in doing the right thing, it's also that her desire to be alone with Henry is motivated by feelings and urges she should rather fight than indulge. Edmund is the only one of the Bertram siblings who is at all considerate of Fanny and her needs, but even that care can fail when it bumps up against his own attraction to Mary Crawford and his desire to cede to her requests: consider Edmund's self-reproach when he lets his liking for Mary prevent him from ensuring Fanny's ability to exercise and thereby be protected from the unreasonable demands of her aunts (*MP* I.7, 87).

The episode of the amateur theatricals unleashes in various members of the family all of these desires and feelings in a sort of maelstrom of self-interest. I should add – not to insist on the priority of biography over fiction – that Austen herself was an enthusiastic participant in this kind of private performance at various stages in her life, and I am personally suspicious of critical arguments that suggest the novel is "against" theatricality and performance in any obvious sense.[3] It seems to me more true to say that when we use something like the occasion of rehearsing a play as a cover story for acting on our own less honorable desires, the play is problematic not because it involves artifice but because acting offers a self-serving alibi for other forms of bad behavior. When Sir Thomas Bertram arrives home unexpectedly, the company is forced to disperse, but he is more an enforcer of correct observance than a deep moralist. Edmund is the only child who receives his father's serious reproach: "He did not enter into any remonstrance with his other children," the narrator adds sardonically: "he was more willing to believe they felt their error, than to run the risk of investigation" (*MP* II.2, 220).

The clearest failure of responsibility during this part of the novel concerns Sir Thomas' failure to take action to prevent the marriage of his older daughter to Mr. Rushworth. Mr. Rushworth is clearly unsuitable; he owns a very considerable property, and his wealth is impressive, but he's neither attractive nor intelligent, and he lacks the substance or even the basic common sense that would render Maria Bertram likely to love, admire and respect him once they are married. Maria clearly has the upper hand already, and verges frequently on expressing a degree of contempt for him that doesn't bode well for their future happiness. But Mr. Rushworth's superficial eligibility is such that Sir Thomas is willing to overlook all of these deficiencies. He rationalizes away the suitor's limitations and, though he offers his daughter the opportunity to back out of a marriage he suspects Maria may not much enjoy, allows himself to be persuaded by her assurances (*MP* II.3, 234–35). She, of course, stung by Henry Crawford's sudden departure (*MP* II.2, 227), angry and mortified, doesn't want to give up any of the consequence – the wealth, the independence – she will achieve by way of marriage to Mr. Rushworth. This is the narrator's verdict on Maria's impatience for that marriage: "In all the important preparations of the mind she was complete; being prepared for matrimony by an hatred of home, restraint, and tranquility; by the misery of disappointed affection, and contempt of the man she was to marry" (*MP* II.3, 236).

This episode serves to set up the return of Henry Crawford, who states almost at once to his sister that during this visit he is going to amuse himself by making Fanny fall in love with him (*MP* II.6, 267). He is oblivious to the depth and extent of Fanny's judgment against him; indeed, Fanny is young and inexperienced, and the novelist may deliberately depict her response to Henry as naïve and hyperbolic rather than quite as well-founded in objective reality as Fanny herself believes. When Henry reminisces that he was never happier than when rehearsing *Lovers' Vows*, it provokes Fanny's harshest judgment. "Never happier!" runs her internal monologue; "—never happier than when doing what you must know was not justifiable!—never happier than when behaving so dishonourably and unfeelingly!—Oh! What a corrupted mind!" (*MP* II.5, 263).

Mansfield Park will go on to offer Fanny a test or temptation in the best tradition of the fairy-tale or mythic archetype; the temptations of Christ in the wilderness may even come to mind, though this test is rendered in a thoroughly secular and familiar mode. Henry Crawford falls in love with Fanny, to his own surprise, and asks her to marry him: a proposal she promptly rejects, to the chagrin of Mansfield Park's other inhabitants. Fanny hopes that telling Sir Thomas that she doesn't like Henry Crawford enough to marry him will satisfy him, but he can't accept that as sufficient, and she feels incapable of telling him what she really knows about Crawford because it would mean uncovering the man's very public flirtations with both of Sir Thomas' own daughters. Henry remains optimistic about his chances with Fanny. He doesn't know that she is in love with Edmund; he just thinks that she's very young (here the narrator gives voice

to Henry's own thoughts in a third-person paraphrase that mixes ventri-
loquism with commentary):

> Must it not follow of course, that when he was understood, he should
> succeed?—he believed it fully. Love such as his, in a man like himself, must
> with perseverance secure a return, and at no great distance; and he had so
> much delight in the idea of obliging her to love him in a very short time, that
> her not loving him now was scarcely regretted. A little difficulty to be
> overcome, was no evil to Henry Crawford. He rather derived spirits from
> it. He had been apt to gain hearts too easily. His situation was new and
> animating. (*MP* III.2, 377)

Given how close these words stay to what must be Henry's own thoughts,
the intensity of the irony is impressive, but it is part of Austen's genius (the
effect will be discussed in greater depth in the next chapter) to manage
identification and judgment at one and the same time. Although Edmund
advises Sir Thomas that time and gratitude will change Fanny's feelings, Sir
Thomas "could not help fearing that if such very long allowances of time
and habit were necessary for her, she might not have persuaded herself into
receiving his addresses properly, before the young man's inclination for
paying them were over" (*MP* III.5, 411).

Supporting the notion that this is a test for Fanny, Sir Thomas decides
to send her home to her own real family in Portsmouth, a decision that
strikes Fanny as painfully generous, given she's no longer in his good
graces, but that really has a different goal:

> His prime motive in sending her away, had very little to do with the
> propriety of her seeing her parents again, and nothing at all with any idea
> of making her happy. He certainly wished her to go willingly, but he as
> certainly wished her to be heartily sick of home before her visit ended; and
> that a little abstinence from the elegancies and luxuries of Mansfield Park,
> would bring her mind into a sober state, and incline her to a juster estimate
> of the value of that home of greater permanence, and equal comfort, of
> which she had the offer.
>
> It was a medicinal project upon his niece's understanding, which he must
> consider as at present diseased. A residence of eight or nine years in the
> abode of wealth and plenty had a little disordered her powers of comparing
> and judging. Her Father's house would, in all probability, teach her the
> value of a good income; and he trusted that she would be the wiser and
> happier woman, all her life, for the experiment he had devised. (*MP* III.6,
> 425–26)

Indeed, though a plot swerve near the end of the novel will save Fanny
from confirming Sir Thomas' suspicions, the effect of immersion in the

squalid, noisy, unpleasant atmosphere of her family home is overwhelming, and everything about the new setting in which Fanny finds herself is conducive to Henry Crawford's suit. When he visits, she introduces him to her crude-mannered father with huge trepidation and painful self-consciousness:

> She could not have a doubt of the manner in which Mr. Crawford must be struck. He must be ashamed and disgusted altogether. He must soon give her up, and cease to have the smallest inclination for the match; and yet, though she had been so much wanting his affection to be cured, this was a sort of cure that would be almost as bad as the complaint; and I believe, there is scarcely a young lady in the united kingdoms, who would not rather put up with the misfortune of being sought by a clever, agreeable man, than have him driven away by the vulgarity of her near relations. (*MP* III.10, 466)

In these settings, indeed, Henry Crawford himself shows to far greater advantage: "She was willing to allow he might have more good qualities than she had been wont to suppose. She began to feel the possibility of his turning out well at last; but he was and must ever be completely unsuited to her, and ought not to think of her" (*MP* 470).

When we read this in light of the novel's ending, we may be skeptical, but several of Austen's siblings are on the record as having hoped that Fanny *would* marry Henry Crawford in the end, and I think Austen's argument is slyer and more subtle than some critics are ready to allow. It is a minor comic refrain, in these pages, that Fanny is being won over by Henry's charm:

> The wonderful improvement which she still fancied in Mr. Crawford, was the nearest to administering comfort of anything within the current of her thoughts. Not considering in how different a circle she had been just seeing him, nor how much might be owing to contrast, she was quite persuaded of his being astonishingly more gentle, and regardful of others, than formerly. (*MP* III.11, 479)

Her naïve extrapolation is that if he is so much kinder now, he will back off from pressing her to marry him: "And if in little things, must it not be so in great? So anxious for her health and comfort, so very feeling as he now expressed himself, and really seemed, might not it be fairly supposed, that he would not much longer persevere in a suit so distressing to her?" (*MP* III.11, 480).

The plot twist here works as a sort of *deus ex machina* – Fanny is saved from the inevitable consequences of her own change of feelings over time by a dramatic external development. First a letter from Mary Crawford desperately tells Fanny to ignore the rumor that Henry Crawford has been spending a good deal of time with the former Maria Bertram (*MP* III.14, 504–05); her subsequent letter alludes to rumors of an elopement and charges Fanny not to believe in it (507). Finally there is actually a paragraph in the newspaper about an elopement; the two names aren't given in full, but the initials of the parties involved and their place of residence are enough to give away their identities. It is Mr. Price who comes across it, shares the information with his family and remarks crudely that if Maria Bertram were his daughter, he'd give her "the rope's end" (he recommends flogging for both the man and the woman in this sort of case (*MP* III.15, 510)).

With this development, both Fanny Price and the forms of Christian morality she has espoused, often to her own cost and with little worldly benefit, are thoroughly vindicated. The final pages of the novel are devoted to a very thorough reckoning with what this means for each of the relevant parties. Sir Thomas is deeply struck by his earlier error concerning Maria's marriage to the unfortunate Mr. Rushworth: "He felt that he ought not to have allowed the marriage, that his daughter's sentiments had been sufficiently known to him to render him culpable in authorizing it, that in so doing he had sacrificed the right to the expedient, and been governed by motives of selfishness and worldly wisdom" (*MP* III.17, 534). He now understands that the effect of his own stringency, in conjunction with Mrs. Norris' flattery of the two girls, was to lead them to hide their real dispositions from him:

> Here had been grievous mismanagement; but, bad as it was, he gradually grew to feel that it had not been the most direful mistake in his plan of education. Something must have been wanting *within*, or time would have worn away much of its ill effect. He feared that principle, active principle, had been wanting, that they had never been properly taught to govern their inclinations and tempers, by that sense of duty which can alone suffice. They had been instructed theoretically in their religion, but never required to bring it into daily practice. To be distinguished for elegance and accomplishments—the authorized object of their youth—could have had no useful influence that way, no moral effect on the mind. He had meant them to be good, but his cares had been directed to the understanding and manners, not the disposition; and of the necessity of self-denial and humility, he feared they had never heard from any lips that could profit them. (*MP* III.17, 536)

But the narrator also explicitly states that Henry's failure to achieve Fanny's hand in marriage is his own fault (implying, in other words, that he would not have been beyond redemption).

If Henry hadn't indulged vanity so far, in terms of reawakening Maria Rushworth's interest in him, "there would have been every probability of success and felicity for him":

> His affection had already done something. Her influence over him had already given him some influence over her. Would he have deserved more, there can be no doubt that more would have been obtained; especially when that marriage had taken place, which would have given him the assistance for her conscience in subduing her first inclination, and brought them very often together. Would he have persevered, and uprightly, Fanny must have been his reward—and a reward very voluntarily bestowed—within a reasonable period from Edmund's marrying Mary. (*MP* III.17, 540)

This passage shows that the novel doesn't paint Henry Crawford as an irredeemable baddie. Like Willoughby, he has been deformed by failures of education and made weak in ways that will be costly to himself as well as to others. It is rather Mrs. Norris who comes across as the novel's worst villain, because of the ways she forces her will on others; she also bears much responsibility for the Bertram daughters' behavior.

In the end, though, none of these characters seems as unequivocally wicked – as destructive and immoral – as the villain of Austen's final novel, *Persuasion*. There we see more clearly than elsewhere in Austen's fiction what she thought a truly immoral person might look like. Mr. Elliot represents a kind of puzzle to Anne. She finds him attractive in many respects, and yet she's wary of his traits. For one thing, he values "rank and connexion" too highly (*P* II.4, 160), but it is more generally true that she can't really get a handle on his real character:

> That he was a sensible man, an agreeable man,—that he talked well, professed good opinions, seemed to judge properly and as a man of principle,–this was all clear enough. He certainly knew what was right, nor could she fix on any one article of moral duty evidently transgressed; but yet she would have been afraid to answer for his conduct. She distrusted the past, if not the present. The names which occasionally dropt of former associates, the allusions to former practices and pursuits, suggested suspicions not favourable of what he had been. She saw that there had been bad habits; that Sunday-travelling had been a common thing; that there had been a period of his life (and probably not a short one) when he had been, at least, careless on all serious matters; and, though he might now think very differently, who could answer for the true sentiments of a clever, cautious man, grown old enough to appreciate a fair character? How could it ever be ascertained that his mind was truly cleansed? (*P* II.5, 174)

Here, then, it's the opacity of his character, his unreadability beneath the obviously superficially attractive manners, that marks him as untrustworthy: "She felt that she could so much more depend upon the sincerity of those who sometimes looked or said a careless thing," the narrator adds, "than of those whose presence of mind never varied, whose tongue never slipped" (*P* II.5, 175).

But the novel doesn't stop here. The revelations from Anne's old school friend about William Elliot's past behavior (especially P II.9, 223) show that he has heartlessly neglected his old friend's impoverished widow, someone whom he would have been in a clear position to help both materially in the first instance and by way of forwarding her business interests overseas in the second. Mrs. Norris may cause more widespread pain by way of her blundering minor malevolence, but William Elliot's decisions and choices are more profoundly immoral, and his character gives us perhaps the clearest sense of what Austen would have seen as the ordinary dimensions of human evil.

CHAPTER 6

Voice

The phrase "free indirect style" was coined to describe a mode of narration that makes only occasional appearances in European fiction before about 1800 but that emerges as one of the novel's most striking formal innovations in the writing of Austen, Flaubert and many of the other great nineteenth- and twentieth-century novelists. In *How Fiction Works*, James Wood helpfully quotes the first sentence of Joyce's great story "The Dead" – "Lily, the caretaker's daughter, was literally run off her feet" – as a clear example of free indirect style, pointing out that "no one is *literally* run off her feet": "What we hear is Lily saying to herself or to a friend (with great emphasis on precisely the most inaccurate word, and with a strong accent): 'Oi was *lit-er-rully* ron off me feet!'"[1]

Free indirect style (the French phrase is *style indirect libre*, and it may also be given in English as "free indirect speech" or "free indirect discourse") is one of a cluster of stylistic tools available to novelists who want to represent characters' inner lives, and Dorrit Cohn's book *Transparent Minds: Narrative Modes for Presenting Consciousness in Fiction* provides the single most exhaustive and intelligent overview of the many different ways in which third-person narrative can integrate the words and thoughts of individual characters. Cohn observes that Austen relies heavily on a technique that Cohn dubs "the narrated monologue," which because it "blurs the line between narration and quotation so dear to the old-fashioned authorial narrator, . . . makes its appearance rather late in the history of narrative genres," at a time when third-person narration "enters the domain previously reserved for first-person (epistolary or confessional) fiction, and begins to focus on the mental and emotional life of its characters."[2] Austen writes exactly on the cusp of this transition, and with regard to Austen's work especially, Claude Rawson prefers the term "free indirect speech" because of the way it foregrounds the distinctive fashion in which the words of an individual character's thoughts or speech migrate into the third-person voice; Rawson observes of free indirect speech that "[i]t combines the ostensibly factual reporting of speech and thought with complex and shifting intimations of judgmental perspective," emphasizing that "[t]he trick is to report actual phrases used, but 'indirectly', so that the narration combines the voice and moral perspective of the original speaker with those of one or more reporting or narrating agents."[3]

It will take a fine touch to distinguish between what I might call ordinary or "bounded" indirect speech and the more elusive phenomenon of free indirect speech. An example from *Pride and Prejudice* will illustrate this point. Mr. Darcy is increasingly attracted to Elizabeth Bennet during her stay at Netherfield: "He really believed, that were it not for the inferiority of her connections, he should be in some danger" (*PP* I.10, 57). This is the narrator restating Darcy's own position. It's not properly free indirect speech, because the verb "believed" acts as a speech verb – or at least a verb of thought – and anchors the entire sentiment in Darcy's mind. But what is the word "really" doing there? Is it Darcy's own adverb, used for emphasis, and if so, does that nudge the sentence into something that at least verges on free indirect speech?

Here is the narrator's follow-up, on Elizabeth's impending departure from Netherfield:

> She attracted him more than he liked—and Miss Bingley was uncivil to *her*, and more teasing than usual to himself. He wisely resolved to be particularly careful that no sign of admiration should *now* escape him, nothing that could elevate her with the hope of influencing his felicity; sensible that if such an idea had been suggested, his behavior during the last day must have material weight in confirming or crushing it. Steady to his purpose, he scarcely spoke ten words to her through the whole of Saturday, and though they were at one time left by themselves for half an hour, he adhered most conscientiously to his book, and would not even look at her. (*PP* I.12, 66)

I wouldn't say that this is exactly free indirect style; the verb "resolved" once again anchors us in Darcy's thoughts, and "wisely" more probably derives from the narrator's perspective than the modifier "really" did in the earlier bit. As the sentence continues, though, more of his words and phrases migrate into the third-person narration ("nothing that could elevate her with the hope of influencing his felicity" – surely this is Darcy's own elevated diction and rather elaborate wording?). Then we zoom back out to the exterior third-person vantage point, which describes Darcy very certainly from the outside – the language about how "he adhered most conscientiously to his book" is not likely to be Darcy's own. It sounds distinctly external in its orientation, and lightly ironized

in a way that comes not from Darcy's own consciousness but from the
narrator's judgmental perspective. The detection of free indirect style is an
art, in other words, not a science, and it will be up to the individual reader
to decide whether it is a useful way of describing the language of consciousness in this particular passage.

Mansfield Park, the novel Austen wrote next after *Pride and Prejudice*,
will help us refine our sense of what this distinctive yet hard-to-pin-down
trait of Austen's narration looks like. The effortless integration of characters' thoughts into the third-person narrative is more striking here, and
the effect generally has more flexibility and range than the relatively
controlled sentences of *Pride and Prejudice* quoted in the previous paragraph. Here, Edmund comes to Fanny's attic to give her a chain on which
to hang her brother's gift of an amber cross; as she's not there, he begins to
write a note, putting it aside when Fanny returns. The note, an insignificant scrap of paper bearing a few words of writing, is to Fanny a treasure:

> It was the only thing approaching to a letter which she had ever received
> from him; she might never receive another; it was impossible that she ever
> should receive another so perfectly gratifying in the occasion and the style.
> Two lines more prized had never fallen from the pen of the most distin-
> guished author—never more completely blessed the researches of the fond-
> est biographer. The enthusiasm of a woman's love is even beyond the
> biographer's. To her, the hand-writing itself, independent of any thing it
> may convey, is a blessedness. Never were such characters cut by any other
> human being, as Edmund's commonest hand-writing gave! This specimen,
> written in haste as it was, had not a fault; and there was a felicity in the flow
> of the first four words, in the arrangement of "My very dear Fanny," which
> she could have looked at forever. (*MP* II.9, 307–08)

It will be very difficult to specify, regarding any single phrase here, where
Fanny's words end and the narrator's begin: this is precisely why it is a good
illustration of free indirect speech. The first and second sentences may be
Fanny's almost exclusively, with the language only moving from what
would have been the first-person present tense in Fanny's thoughts ("It is
the only thing . . . I have . . .; I might . . . ") to the third person and the past
tense. But with the words "it was impossible" we feel, imperceptibly, the
narrator's voice and judgment begin to overlay Fanny's language.

Fanny herself has probably just thought something more like "I will
never again receive such a perfectly gratifying letter from him"; the phrase
"it was impossible that" starts to sound as though it must be the narrator's
construction, though, and the following sentence even more strongly
moves us into the narrator's perspective – or does it? Are these words

marked with the narrator's irony, Fanny's own hyperbole, or perhaps a bit of both? The accumulation of clauses – "never fallen . . . never . . . blessed" – and the move into a mode of pronouncement ("The enthusiasm . . . ") feel narratorial, they do not plausibly derive from Fanny's own consciousness, and yet the language continues to feature strings of words that sound like Fanny ("Never were such characters cut . . . "), and even what seems almost like a slip of the pen, the present-tense "is" in the phrase "is a blessedness," which by Austen's own usual practice (cued by the third-personization of "To her") should be conjugated in the past tense "was." Words like "specimen" and "felicity" seem more likely to originate in the narrator's playful use of elevated diction, and yet they could still emerge from Fanny's own lexicon. In sum, this passage displays the deep intermingling of an individual character's words and thoughts with a third-person narrative voice that swoops in and out of that character's consciousness at will.

The quality of ironic judgment or summing-up very frequently colors Austen's practice of free indirect style. Here is another passage of interest. It features some irony at Fanny's expense, even as her own words are given in a form that we suspect must be close to verbatim, and it is again very difficult to determine where Fanny's words stop and the narrator's take over. Fanny is steeling herself for the possibility that she will receive a letter from Edmund announcing his engagement to Mary Crawford:

> For this letter she must try to arm herself. That a letter from Edmund should be a subject of terror! She began to feel that she had not yet gone through all the changes of opinion and sentiment, which the progress of time and variation of circumstances occasion in this world of changes. The vicissitudes of the human mind had not yet been exhausted by her. (*MP* III.6, 431)

The first two sentences hew fairly closely still to Fanny's own line of thought and have the feel of her own words, while the third sentence then re-anchors us albeit indirectly in her own thought or speech ("She began to feel . . . "). The rest of the thought is probably still Fanny's. What about the final sentence, though? The passive construction is striking, and the word "vicissitudes" again has that quality of elevated diction, suggesting a slight ironization, a possible narratorial intervention in the direction of judgment. But there are no definite answers concerning subtle flavors of narration.

Elsewhere, we see more clearly how the narrative borrows and frames Fanny's own thoughts in order to ironize them or undermine them by exposing their hyperbolic nature. Fanny's response to the elopement of Henry Crawford and Maria Rushworth, for instance, takes place in a register the third-person narration doesn't completely endorse. We are very close to Fanny's thoughts here, and yet we are also in a space of judgment that distances us from them, so that we are more likely to judge her naïve or excessively shocked than to endorse her feelings on the occasion:

> Sir Thomas's parental solicitude, and high sense of honour and decorum, Edmund's upright principles, unsuspicious temper, and genuine strength of feeling, made her think it scarcely possible for them to support life and reason under such disgrace; and it appeared to her, that as far as this world alone was concerned, the greatest blessing to every one of kindred with Mrs. Rushworth would be instant annihilation. (*MP* III.15, 511)

An illuminating contrast can be drawn between the moments of subtle narratorial judgment that tend to cluster around passages of free indirect style and a set of more direct narratorial intrusions. An Austen narrator, invisible most of the time, probably can't be thought of as having either a gender or an age (or indeed the less easily enumerated qualities of "personhood"), but has a voice that sharpens sometimes into a persona of sorts, at least to the point of sometimes using the personal pronoun "I." Henry Fielding is Austen's great predecessor here. Fielding's novel *Tom Jones* (1749) represents a masterwork in terms of the development of a brilliantly intrusive authorial persona. The novel features a narrator who explicitly identifies himself as an author, with all of the preening and self-involvement that might suggest, and the narrator's digressions and pontifications form almost as much the meat or drama of the book as the story of the incidents that affect Tom Jones himself. Fielding's narrator "warns" us early on that this will be the case:

> Reader, I think proper, before we proceed any farther together, to acquaint thee, that I intend to digress, through this whole History, as often as I see Occasion: Of which I am myself a better Judge than any pitiful Critic whatever. And here I must desire all those Critics to mind their own Business, and not to intermeddle with Affairs, or Works, which no ways concern them: For, till they produce the Authority by which they are constituted Judges, I shall plead to their Jurisdiction.[4]

Indeed, intrusive narration forms such an essential and characteristic part of *Tom Jones* that critic Wayne Booth once suggested that the novel's "running account of growing intimacy between the narrator and the reader" is "a kind of plot of its own," with its own "separate denouement."[5]

Austen's narrators aren't usually so prominent as Fielding's, but they do foreground themselves periodically to offer judgment and summing-up of a more explicit kind than can be accomplished in stretches like the passages of free indirect style quoted in the preceding pages. Look, for instance, at this comment from the narrator. It falls immediately after a conversation in which Henry Crawford tells his sister that he wants to make Fanny Price fall in love with him. She suggests that this wouldn't be kind but doesn't say much more than that:

> And without attempting any further remonstrance, she left Fanny to her fate—a fate which, had not Fanny's heart been guarded in a way unsuspected by Miss Crawford, might have been a little harder than she deserved; for although there doubtless are such unconquerable young ladies of eighteen (or one should not read about them) as are never to be persuaded into love against their judgment by all that talent, manner, attention, and flattery can do, I have no inclination to believe Fanny one of them, or to think that with so much tenderness of disposition, and so much taste as belonged to her, she could have escaped heart-whole from the courtship (though the courtship only of a fortnight) of such a man as Crawford, in spite of there being some previous ill-opinion of him to be overcome, had not her affection been engaged elsewhere. (*MP* II.6, 270)

There is something arch or coy about the phrase "young ladies of eighteen," and the same quality inheres in some of the subsequent locutions, but the stylized nature of the voice is partly what licenses it to make such a positive pronouncement about the main character. It is a moment of partisanship and advocacy (Fanny's "tenderness of disposition" and "taste" are singled out unequivocally for praise), and the narrator's certainty about Fanny's real nature is matched by equal certainty concerning counterfactual scenarios, with the narrator confidently making accurate predictions about what would come to pass under a different set of conditions.

The chapter on revision lays out some of the advantages of looking to Austen's earliest works to identify techniques that will come to be executed less conspicuously in the later works. For Austen's early development of the intrusive narrator, *Northanger Abbey* provides the clearest and fullest evidence. This short novel was published only posthumously, in two volumes alongside the other two volumes of Austen's final completed novel *Persuasion*, but it was composed and completed in the first years of the new century under the title *Susan* (at that stage, the name of the female protagonist), with only relatively small changes made later when it was revised for publication. This is Catherine Tilney agonizing about what to wear to the cotillion ball at the Pump Room, and the sound of the narrator

here (pompous, pontificating) is much more strongly reminiscent of
Fielding's intrusive narrators than anything we can "hear" in Austen's
later novels:

> What gown and what head-dress she should wear on the occasion became
> her chief concern. She cannot be justified in it. Dress is at all times
> a frivolous distinction, and excessive solicitude about it often destroys its
> own aim. Catherine knew all this very well; her great aunt had read her
> a lecture on the subject only the Christmas before; and yet she lay awake
> ten minutes on Wednesday night debating between her spotted and her
> tamboured muslin, and nothing but the shortness of the time prevented
> her buying a new one for the evening. This would have been an error in
> judgment, great though not uncommon, from which one of the other sex
> rather than her own, a brother rather than a great aunt might have warned
> her, for man only can be aware of the insensibility of man towards a new
> gown. It would be mortifying to the feelings of many ladies, could they be
> made to understand how little the heart of man is affected by what is costly
> or new in their attire; how little it is biased by the texture of their muslin,
> and how unsusceptible of peculiar tenderness towards the spotted, the
> sprigged, the mull or the jackonet. Woman is fine for her own satisfaction
> alone. No man will admire her the more, no woman will like her the better
> for it. Neatness and fashion are enough for the former, and a something of
> shabbiness or impropriety will be most endearing to the latter.—But not
> one of these grave reflections troubled the tranquillity of Catherine.
> (NA I.10, 71)

This is more exuberant, less controlled than the elegant satirical flourishes
of *Pride and Prejudice* or *Emma*. The impersonation of a moralizing,
pontificating narrator produces an extended and extravagant tongue-in-
cheek meditation on the frivolity of dress that in turn segues into a musing
on the relative priorities of dress to men and to women, leading to the
grand aphoristic generalization, "Woman is fine for her own satisfaction
alone," then the ironic deflation of tone as we move back to Catherine's
obliviousness. This narrative arabesque really can't come from Catherine's
consciousness.

Northanger Abbey can help us understand a number of other techniques and properties in Austen's later novels. Austen is clearly already
interested in experimenting with gaps between what a character knows
and what is known to the narrator, to the reader or in some sense even
just knowable within the world or consciousness of the novel as
a whole. Catherine's naïveté licenses fairly radical experimentation
with the tension between incomprehension and knowingness. She is
bemused, for instance, by why the presence of General Tilney so

strongly inhibits the enjoyment of herself and his children, even as his bad temper and controlling behavior give the reader an evident explanation (*NA* II.1, 131). I would call this a precursor to free indirect style rather than the full-blown version of the later novels, but the narrator slips very readily into Catherine's consciousness, ventriloquizing her thoughts in a way that invites the reader to assume a position not of identification but of ironic distance. Here is a good example:

> The Tilneys, they, by whom above all, she desired to be favourably thought of, outstripped even her wishes in the flattering measures by which their intimacy was to be continued. She was to be their chosen visitor, she was to be for weeks under the same roof with the person whose society she mostly prized—and, in addition to all the rest, this roof was to be the roof of an abbey!—Her passion for ancient edifices was next in degree to her passion for Henry Tilney—and castles and abbies made usually the charm of those reveries which his image did not fill. To see and explore either the ramparts and keep of the one, or the cloisters of the other, had been for many weeks a darling wish, though to be more than the visitor of an hour, had seemed too nearly impossible for desire. And yet, this was to happen. (*NA* II.2, 143)

The transposition of Catherine's own thoughts into a third-person perspective automatically produces irony at Catherine's expense. There is little difficulty here putting a finger on the relationship between the character's words and the narrator's point of view, which are curiously at once nearly convergent and markedly distinct:

> It was wonderful that her friends should seem so little elated by the possession of such a home; that the consciousness of it should be so meekly born. The power of early habit only could account for it. A distinction to which they had been born gave no pride. Their superiority of abode was no more to them than their superiority of person. (*NA* II.2, 144)

As these sentences accumulate, we are ever more deeply struck by Catherine's painful and comic naïveté, the silliness of her understanding of the world and the gap between her perceptions and reality-based thinking.

Here is another good example of how *close* the third-person narration remains to Catherine's own line of thought, with the reader's judgment enabled not by the swooping-in-and-out summing-up power of free indirect style but by simple paraphrase into the third person. Catherine is reacting to the relegation of the late Mrs. Tilney's portrait to Eleanor's bedroom, General Tilney having deemed the painting not well-enough executed for the drawing room:

> Catherine attempted no longer to hide from herself the nature of the feelings
> which, in spite of all his attentions, he had previously excited; and what had
> been terror and dislike before, was now absolute aversion. Yes, aversion! His
> cruelty to such a charming woman made him odious to her. She had often
> read of such characters; characters, which Mr. Allen had been used to call
> unnatural and overdrawn; but here was proof positive of the contrary.
> (*NA* II.7, 185–86)

That said, while her positive hyperbole is mostly laughable, Catherine's
equally exaggerated instincts about the dangers of her situation are not
altogether off target. Her vocabulary is overblown, certainly, and some of
the humor is still at Catherine's expense, but there is another layer to the
joking, which is to say that General Tilney *does* have a streak of cruelty,
even if it is "merely" the temper that leads his children to tread warily lest
they arouse his anger. Here, the passage starts with a verb clause that
anchors us in Catherine's actual thoughts ("attempted no longer to
hide") before moving into something like indirect speech.

Quotation marks are not used to bracket these thoughts, but elsewhere
Austen will use them explicitly to mark a character's thinking. In our own
time, convention has hardened such that the words within the quotation
marks are supposed to be exactly what the character has uttered; in the early
nineteenth century, though, such conventions had not yet solidified, and
Austen sometimes rephrases such thoughts in the third person (this is
treated at greater length in Chapter 3, "Revision"). This would be
a typical example:

> An hour passed away before the General came in, spent, on the part of his
> young guest, in no very favourable consideration of his character.—"This
> lengthened absence, these solitary rambles, did not speak a mind at ease, or
> a conscience void of reproach." (*NA* II.8, 187)

Those are Catherine's thoughts within the inverted commas, but they have
moved from present to past tense just as they would move from first- to
third-person voice if there were pronouns in the case. The key point here is
that the narrator first anchors us in a scene of Catherine thinking and only
then gives us the words that run through her mind, words that echo the
cant of literature and hold a hint of that high-flown diction that often
discredits or partially ironizes the original sentiment.

It is not a subtle effect. The novel features a string of such episodes, and
similar verbal symptoms can be seen in a passage that follows shortly
afterward. When Catherine is called back from the gallery she is about to
enter, the discouragement to exploration piques her curiosity:

> Something was certainly to be concealed; her fancy, though it had trespassed lately once or twice, could not mislead her here; and what that something was, a short sentence of Miss Tilney's, as they followed the General at some distance down stairs, seemed to point out:—"I was going to take you into what was my mother's room—the room in which she died—" were all her words; but few as they were, they conveyed pages of intelligence to Catherine. It was no wonder that the General should shrink from the sight of such objects as that room must contain; a room in all probability never entered by him since the dreadful scene had passed, which released his suffering wife, and left him to the stings of conscience. (*NA* II.8, 191)

Not long after this, Catherine's misperceptions are cleared up by Henry Tilney's intervention. It features some of the details concerning body language that I wrote about in the chapter on conversation; the scene mostly consists of the words actually spoken by Henry and Catherine to each other, with the narrator merely noting minor details of delivery to bring the characters' manner more vividly to life. Catherine's allusion to Mrs. Tilney's sudden death is marked merely with the words "slowly, and with hesitation it was spoken"; Austen provides no pronoun, just a passive construction and a few adverbial modifiers. The narrator continues to offer these delicate notations:

> "And from these circumstances," he replied (his quick eye fixed on her's), "you infer perhaps the probability of some negligence—some—(involuntarily she shook her head)—or it may be—of something still less pardonable." (*NA* II.9, 202)

This use of punctuation marks as an impressionistic gesture, rather than as a literal guide to which words are spoken by a character and which added by the impersonal narrator, was relatively common in eighteenth-century fiction, though today it would represent a breach in the rules of punctuation.

Catherine is now awakened to truth, in a fashion that clearly resembles subsequent moments of realization in *Pride and Prejudice* and *Emma*, the heroine coming face to face with her own profound misunderstanding of people and situations. The language here is simpler and more hyperbolic, though, with the main effect still being a sort of sympathetic comedy at Catherine's expense:

> The visions of romance were over. Catherine was completely awakened. Henry's address, short as it had been, had more thoroughly opened her eyes to the extravagance of her late fancies than all their several disappointments had done. Most grievously was she humbled. Most bitterly did she cry. It was not only with herself that she was sunk—but with Henry. Her folly,

which now seemed even criminal, was all exposed to him, and he must
despise her for ever. The liberty which her imagination had dared to take
with the character of his father, could he ever forgive it? The absurdity of her
curiosity and her fears, could they ever be forgotten? She hated herself more
than she could express. (*NA* II.10, 204)

The degree of Austen's enjoyment of this opportunity for comedy is
suggested by the fact that the treatment of Catherine's change of heart is
so protracted.

More of it, in a passage that is one of the intellectual and aesthetic
centers of the book, can be found here – look out as you read for the
interplay between the third-person narrator's voice and Catherine's own
thoughts (I would say that this is more subtle than some of the earlier
examples from *Northanger Abbey*, and that the language more clearly
anticipates some of the effects we find most striking and original in the
later fiction):

Charming as were all Mrs. Radcliffe's works, and charming even as were the
works of all her imitators, it was not in them perhaps that human nature, at
least in the midland counties of England, was to be looked for. Of the Alps
and Pyrenees, with their pine forests and their vices, they might give
a faithful delineation; and Italy, Switzerland, and the South of France,
might be as fruitful in horrors as they were there represented. Catherine
dared not doubt beyond her own country, and even of that, if hard pressed,
would have yielded the northern and western extremities. But in the central
part of England there was surely some security for the existence even of
a wife not beloved, in the laws of the land, and the manners of the age.
Murder was not tolerated, servants were not slaves, and neither poison nor
sleeping potions to be procured, like rhubarb, from every druggist.
(*NA* II.10, 205)

And yet it is important to reiterate that Catherine's suspicions of General
Tilney will be in some fundamental sense vindicated by the plot. Novel
cant is also truth: when General Tilney finds out that he has been misled
concerning Catherine's fortune, he sends her home without ceremony,
indeed without even a servant to accompany her and without making sure
she has enough money to pay her way (*NA* II.13, 231). When this misunderstanding and its sequel are later unfolded to Catherine by Henry,
indeed, the narrator affectionately samples another moment of Catherine's
characteristic hyperbole: "Catherine, at any rate, heard enough to feel, that
in suspecting General Tilney of either murdering or shutting up his wife,
she had scarcely sinned against his character, or magnified his cruelty"
(*NA* II.15, 256).

Free indirect style and the effects it enables – subtle probing of an individual character's interior life, the perspective of judgment but not at the cost of imaginative identification or empathy – are strongly but subtly present throughout *Pride and Prejudice*, but it is *Emma* where the narrative voice achieves the most sublime apotheosis of self-aggrandizement (Emma's) in conjunction with self-abnegation (the narrator's). Austen's sentences often have a certain aphoristic flair (think of the famous opening line of *Pride and Prejudice*), but *Emma*'s prose style regularly and deliberately sets aphorisms into narrative, the static aspect of aphoristic summing-up poised in dynamic tension with the forward momentum of storytelling. D. A. Miller points out that although readers tend to assume that the "perfection" of what he calls "Austen Style" is "highest, most visible and delectable, in bite-size form," actual maxims are very infrequent in her fiction: although "Austen's narration may still be thought to sustain as a whole the all-sufficiency of the epigrams that only sporadically spangle its pages," he asserts, the relationship between Austen Style and storytelling must nonetheless be one of denial, incompleteness, lack.[6]

There are a number of moments in *Emma* when an aphorism bursts forth in glorious freestanding isolation, and can be quoted more or less independently. It is never clear whether such formulations are Emma's own or whether they derive instead from the consciousness of that impersonal narrator, and the fact that a hard and fast answer to the question can't really be achieved speaks to exactly what's so intriguing about free indirect style. This is the novel's verdict on the visit from Emma's sister and brother-in-law and their children: "She had nothing to wish otherwise, but that the days did not pass so swiftly. It was a delightful visit;–perfect, in being much too short" (*E* I.13, 116). And again, consider this maxim about the gap between expectations and reality in advance of the visit to Box Hill: "Nothing was wanting but to be happy when they got there" (*E* III.7, 399).

The narrative rules of *Emma* allow for a maxim sometimes to be elaborated into something that allows for a momentary pause for the contemplation of character, almost like the prose "characters" of important historical figures that punctuate the narrative histories of Hume and Gibbon. Here, anyway, is the narrator's summing-up of Captain Weston's first marriage, with the former Miss Churchill:

> It was an unsuitable connection, and did not produce much happiness. Mrs. Weston ought to have found more in it, for she had a husband whose warm heart and sweet temper made him think every thing due to her in return for the great goodness of being in love with him; but though she had one sort of spirit, she had not the best. She had resolution enough to pursue

her own will in spite of her brother, but not enough to refrain from unreasonable regrets at that brother's unreasonable anger, nor from missing the luxuries of her former home. They lived beyond their income, but still it was nothing in comparison of Enscombe: she did not cease to love her husband, but she wanted at once to be the wife of Captain Weston, and Miss Churchill of Enscombe. (*E* I.2, 13–14)

The structure of the sentences invokes ideas of balance and equipoise, although beneath the superficial stasis lurks a sense of instability and disproportion. The distinction between "one sort of spirit" and "the best" (the words "sort of spirit" don't need to be repeated for clarity, of course, but their omission the second time round contributes to the sentence's stylized or aphoristic feel) introduces a devastating judgment.

Look at the structure of the two following sentences, too – "She had resolution enough to . . ., but not enough to refrain from . . ., nor from . . . " – the clauses are nested, with the second "nor" clause coming off the subordinate pronoun "from" rather than running in parallel to the sentence's main verb. That sentence has one main prong and two subsidiary ones, making a total of three important elements; the final sentence is built out of an even number of components rather than an odd one, with the implicitly destabilizing feel of the odd number of clauses rounded out and rebalanced by the double assertions of the final sentence. Each one is balanced by a "but," and the two observations are put in apposition by way of a colon in the middle (it could perhaps equally well have been a semi-colon, though I think the colon is more dynamic). There is a subsidiary piece of balancing in the setting of the two different named identities against each other in the last line of the paragraph – "the wife of Captain Weston," "Miss Churchill of Enscombe" – it is a sentence that an anthropologist from Mars might find bewildering, or that any rate only makes sense in light of extensive knowledge concerning this society's beliefs about gender, marriage and social status, but then Austen's fiction is in some meaningful sense designed precisely to educate the reader in such matters by delineating them with proto-sociological precision.

In the passage just quoted, there is no particular reason to credit Emma Woodhouse with the core observation, though it is certainly plausible to think that she would endorse such an analysis. Elsewhere in the novel, Emma's voice can heard with more strength and distinctiveness. The transposition of Emma's thoughts into the third-person narration, and the delicate balance between identification and external judgment, comes through clearly and frequently in the novel's pages, with a particularly good example occurring in this sequence of sentences about Harriet Smith's disappointment in the matter of Mr. Elton:

> Her tears fell abundantly—but her grief was so truly artless, that no dignity could have made it more respectable in Emma's eyes—and she listened to her and tried to console her with all her heart and understanding—really for the time convinced that Harriet was the superior creature of the two—and that to resemble her would be more for her own welfare and happiness than all that genius or intelligence could do.
>
> It was rather too late in the day to set about being simple-minded and ignorant; but she left her with every previous resolution confirmed of being humble and discreet, and repressing imagination all the rest of her life. (*E* I.17, 153)

The adjective "respectable" here has all of its original force. Emma genuinely respects Harriet's grief; it is characteristic of an older generation of eighteenth-century prose stylists to use words, sometimes but not always Latinate, in their root sense, so that when historian Edward Gibbon calls another writer's work "laborious" he's not insulting it, just saying that it took a great deal of effort to compile. We also can see the intensifier "really" working here to help us swoop with the narrator into Emma's own consciousness, until we come to hear her words almost from the inside. "To resemble Harriet would be more for my own welfare and happiness than all that genius or intelligence can do," we might imagine Emma thinking to herself, in pretty much those exact words.

With the terms "genius" and "intelligence," though, we pivot back from sensibility toward satire. Both terms are hyperbolic, and the next sentence (it begins a new paragraph, and the break gives the words additional force) has already become exaggerated to the point of admitting its own implausibility. There is a hint of sarcasm in the idea of it being too late "to set about being simple-minded and ignorant" (nobody could really consider this desirable), and a strongly comic effect is produced in the final clause by Emma's determination to achieve something altogether and intrinsically incompatible with her own traits and tendencies. That phrase "repressing imagination," by the way, will be picked up later in the novel when Emma is referred to (it may be her own coinage for her peculiar form of social artistry, the discerning of connections and affinities between others) as an "imaginist" (*E* III.3, 362), with a final comic-satirical twist coming when the novel demonstrates that rather than calling things into being with her imagination, as she intends, Emma has actually merely imagined things that are not real.

The sharpness of the sarcasm we hear in that first line of the second paragraph is partly a function of discontinuity or break. We are highly aware of the sudden change of tone, and Austen trains us as readers to attend to such changes of mode, with it being habitual in Austen's fiction that the reader is first alerted to an emotional response or an intellectual argument by way of some movement of style or diction. Consider this sentence in *Emma*, which describes Jane Fairfax having reached the age at which she thinks she should start earning her living as a governess: "With the fortitude of a devoted noviciate, she had resolved at one-and-twenty to complete the sacrifice, and retire from all the pleasures of life, of rational intercourse, equal society, peace and hope, to penance and mortification for ever" (*E* II.2, 176). Is the hyperbole Jane's own? If so, is there something self-ironizing about it? Or is it the narrator's irony, which would come more at Jane's expense? Even becoming a governess cannot really be one permanent stream of penance and mortification, or deprive one altogether of rational discourse and the society of one's equals.

A radical critique of women's fates and fortunes in this period can be found in Mary Wollstonecraft's *Vindication of the Rights of Woman* (1792), a book that we don't know whether or not Austen read but whose ideas had migrated sufficiently into the larger conversations of the 1790s that she would at least have been familiar with its title and main arguments. There is an oblique allusion to the title in *Emma*, one so glancing that we must think of it as being deliberately, even obtusely apolitical: "Mrs. Weston proposed having no regular supper; merely sandwiches, &c. set out in the little room; but that was scouted as a wretched suggestion. A private dance, without sitting down to supper, was pronounced an infamous fraud upon the rights of men and women" (*E* II.11, 273).

That is not to say that the novel doesn't give voice, at times, to arguments about the vulnerability of young middle-class women who need to earn their livings. Jane Fairfax makes a pained reference (she is trying to be satirical, one suspects, but it must be a self-protective irony) to the inquiry offices where someone like herself will seek work, calling them "Offices for the sale—not quite of human flesh—but of human intellect," an allusion that her friend Mrs. Elton takes personally in a way that Jane didn't mean, suggesting defensively that her own brother-in-law, merchant though he may be, is not pro-slave trade but rather "a friend of abolition" (*E* II.17, 325). In response, Jane disclaims any intention to take a position on the slave trade: "governess-trade, I assure you, was all that I had in view; widely different certainly as to the guilt of those who carry it on; but as to the greater misery of the victims, I do not know where it lies" (*E* II.17, 325).

This sidestep is also characteristic of the ways that Austen's novels dodge taking a stance on public matters of political import, mostly borrowing the languages of rights, property and slavery to comment more narrowly on the condition of women in a particular social milieu.

One of the effects I've always found most attractive in Austen's fiction concerns the prevalence of ironic sentences that are largely unanchored in an individual character's consciousness, though they have the "feel" of a personal comment. *Emma* is full of sentences in which lurking irony becomes outright irony. Here is one of my favorite examples: "After being long fed with hopes of a speedy visit from Mr. and Mrs. Suckling, the Highbury world were obliged to endure the mortification of hearing that they could not possibly come till the autumn. No such importation of novelties could enrich their intellectual stores at present" (*E* III.6, 382). That initial verb "fed" already underlines the preposterous nature of the idea that there would be something nourishing to the community about a visit from this couple (their name invokes the "suckling pig" of feastdom), and the sentence that follows takes the diction up a notch and restates the assertion even more preposterously.

A similar effect can be found later in the same chapter when Mr. Knightley deems it important, if the hypochondriac Mr. Woodhouse is to dine with them at Donwell, to have the meal served indoors: "He was invited on good faith," the narrator proceeds. "No lurking horrors were to upbraid him for his easy credulity" (*E* III.6, 387). Again, the hyperbole of the second sentence can't really come from Mr. Woodhouse's own consciousness – he is neither so verbally acute nor so self-aware. We feel instead a certain narratorial relish at the sheer power and possibilities of language, at what happens when an obvious thought or sentiment is restated in sharper, more elevated diction that implicitly turns its effects toward satire.

Though satire is less strongly present at the large-scale level in *Persuasion* than it is in *Emma*, it remains an effect that can be strongly locally invoked, even as the novel maintains a high degree of stylistic command. The opening paragraphs of *Persuasion* are worth a very close look, as is the handling of the physical transition of Anne and Lady Russell to Bath, which uses a technique much like the "dissolve" of film to achieve an extraordinarily graceful and economical elision of time and space.[7] Here, though, I'll focus on the integration of satirical modes and satirical judgments into a novel that is generally acknowledged to be sadder and more subdued in its tone than any of Austen's prior ones.

I am especially interested in the language the novel uses around the question of how one speaks and feels about a dead family member. Mrs. Musgrove is genuinely moved by grief when she thinks of her lost son Dick – his life and death have been brought to mind by the presence of Captain Wentworth, who was Dick's lieutenant on one of his ships – but the novel significantly ironizes that sentiment, as well as the sorts of conventional speech and thinking that push us toward false pieties at the expense of honest description:

> The real circumstances of this pathetic piece of family history were, that the Musgroves had had the ill fortune of a very troublesome, hopeless son; and the good fortune to lose him before he reached his twentieth year; that he had been sent to sea, because he was stupid and unmanageable on shore; that he had been very little cared for at any time by his family, though quite as much as he deserved; seldom heard of, and scarcely at all regretted, when the intelligence of his death abroad had worked its way to Uppercross, two years before.
>
> He had, in fact, though his sisters were now doing all they could for him, by calling him "poor Richard," been nothing better than a thick-headed, unfeeling, unprofitable Dick Musgrove, who had never done any thing to entitle himself to more than the abbreviation of his name, living or dead. (*P* I.6, 54)

This passage is ruthless in its disavowal of sentiment. Anti-sentimentality represents a strong strain throughout Austen's fiction, highly visible in the unpublished works of her childhood and adolescence but strong, too, at moments like this one. (She is skeptical especially about false idealizations of children – think of the devastating account offered in the opening pages of *Sense and Sensibility* of how the sentiment surrounding a small grandson can displace the rights of grown-up daughters.)

Mrs. Musgrove's grief for her son will be elaborated in a subsequent scene whose other significance is that it seats Anne and Captain Wentworth together on a single sofa for the first time since their long estrangement, "divided only by Mrs. Musgrove," as the narrator notes:

> It was no insignificant barrier indeed. Mrs. Musgrove was of a comfortable substantial size, infinitely more fitted by nature to express good cheer and good humour, than tenderness and sentiment; and while the agitations of Anne's slender form, and pensive face, may be considered as very completely screened, Captain Wentworth should be allowed some credit for the self-command with which he attended to her large fat sighings over the destiny of a son, whom alive nobody had cared for.

> Personal size and mental sorrow have certainly no necessary proportions. A large bulky figure has as good a right to be in deep affliction, as the most graceful set of limbs in the world. But, fair or not fair, there are unbecoming conjunctions, which reason will patronize in vain,—which taste cannot tolerate,—which ridicule will seize. (*P* I.8, 73–74)

Mrs. Musgrove is far from being the only character at whose expense *Persuasion*'s narrator has fun. Even Anne, as protectively as the novel treats her, will be subject to narrative irony, as when she refuses to speculate, late in the novel, as to how she might have felt about Mr. Elliot's suit (she has not yet had the conversation with her friend Mrs. Smith in which she will be apprised of his deep-dyed villainy) had there been "no Captain Wentworth in the case" (*P* II.9, 208). It is moot because whether or not it is possible for Anne to marry the captain, "her affection would be his for ever": "Their union, she believed, could not divide her more from other men, than their final separation," the narrator says.

Think about exactly what's being said here. Anne believes she will be no less permanently cut off from marriage with another man if she and Wentworth never see each other again than if the two of them were to get married after all: a strong line to take, and rather reminiscent of Fanny Price's misconceived conviction that she could never marry Henry Crawford. And what about the next paragraph? After the serious, almost tragic dipping-in to Anne's thoughts, the narrator swoops back out and offers this two-sentence comment: "Prettier musings of high-wrought love and eternal constancy, could never have passed along the streets of Bath, than Anne was sporting with from Camden-place to Westgate-buildings. It was almost enough to spread purification and perfume along the way" (*P* II.9, 208). I find it psychologically implausible that these are Anne's own words and thoughts; Anne is self-aware but she isn't habitually sarcastic. The sarcasm seems to derive chiefly from the narrator.

In the essay "No One Is Alone" (one of the pieces that makes up the brilliant book *Jane Austen, or The Secret of Style*), D. A. Miller identifies "the staring paradox of Austen's narration" as being that "it is at once utterly exempt from the social necessities that govern the narrated world, and intimately acquainted with them down to their most subtle psychic effects on character" (32). One of the places where something interesting always happens in terms of the coalescing of a disembodied narrator into a personified "I" comes with the proposal of marriage that falls near the end of every one of Austen's published novels. It is almost as though there is a secret rule, a convention that must be followed, that the narrator shifts at this juncture into provisional personhood in order to – to do what? It has something to do with privacy or decorum, the need to protect the female protagonist especially from the glare of publicity and watching eyes, drawing off attention that might be damaging or intrusive, and in the last bit of this chapter, I want to look at each of those moments in turn for what they can cumulatively tell us about the narrative persona and voice of Austen's fiction.

I'll take *Northanger Abbey* first. The proposal of marriage is not narrated directly and the narrator becomes briefly Fieldingesque in his or her willingness (I have asked this already, but is it possible to ascribe a gender to these narrators?) to pontificate about human nature and morality. Part of the point here is to provide a slightly debunking explanation for why it is that Henry Tilney fell in love with Catherine to begin with. Look at the language:

> Some explanation on his father's account he had to give; but his first purpose was to explain himself, and before they reached Mr. Allen's grounds he had done it so well, that Catherine did not think it could ever be repeated too often. She was assured of his affection; and that heart in return was solicited, which, perhaps, they pretty equally knew was already entirely his own; for, though Henry was now sincerely attached to her, though he felt and delighted in all the excellencies of her character and truly loved her society, I must confess that his affection originated in nothing better than gratitude, or, in other words, that a persuasion of her partiality for him had been the only cause of giving her a serious thought. It is a new circumstance in romance, I acknowledge, and dreadfully derogatory of an heroine's dignity; but if it be as new in common life, the credit of a wild imagination will at least be all my own. (*NA* II.15, 252–53)

The corresponding scene in *Sense and Sensibility* already suggests that the convention of not "particularly" narrating the interaction has hardened into a firm constraint. This is the relevant passage describing Edward Ferrars' proposal to Elinor:

> How soon he had walked himself into the proper resolution, however, how soon an opportunity of exercising it occurred, in what manner he expressed himself, and how he was received, need not be particularly told. This only need be said;–that when they all sat down to table at four o'clock, about three hours after his arrival, he had secured his lady, engaged her mother's consent, and was not only in the rapturous profession of the lover, but in the reality of reason and truth, one of the happiest of men. (*SS* III.13, 409)

The passage gestures toward its own unwillingness to particularize; it also uses a language of convention that may be aligned with "the reality of reason and truth," but that again shields the lovers by dint of its sheer generic nature. There is an addendum to the *Sense and Sensibility* proposal, moreover, as the narrator recaps all of the events that led up to the proposal:

> ... He could do nothing till he were assured of his fate with Miss Dashwood; and by his rapidity in seeking *that* fate, it is to be supposed, in spite of the jealousy with which he had once thought of Colonel Brandon, in spite of the modesty with which he rated his own deserts, and the politeness with which he talked of his doubts, he did not, upon the whole, expect a very cruel reception. It was his business, however, to say that he *did*, and he said it very prettily. What he might say on the subject a twelvemonth after, must be referred to the imagination of husbands and wives. (*SS* 415)

It is almost coy, this unwillingness to specify words, and I think the effect of the last two sentences is to distance us from the immediacy of the scene of proposal, curiously or perversely actually bringing alive the real private protected future intimacy of marriage a year in.

These scenes create a pattern whose minor variations may also tell us something about how Austen's priorities and goals would change over time, or at least in response to the imperatives of a given plot and set of characters. *Pride and Prejudice* yet again expresses playfulness on the one hand about convention and on the other about the history a reader brings to the end of a new novel by a familiar novelist (remember that the title page didn't give Austen's name, just saying that the book was "By the Author of 'Sense and Sensibility'"). Darcy has proposed to Elizabeth, and this is how the narrator handles her response:

> Elizabeth feeling all the more than common awkwardness and anxiety of his situation, now forced herself to speak; and immediately, though not very fluently, gave him to understand, that her sentiments had undergone so material a change, since the period to which he alluded, as to make her receive with gratitude and pleasure, his present assurances. The happiness which this reply produced, was such as he had probably never felt before; and he expressed himself on the occasion as sensibly and as warmly as a man violently in love can be supposed to do. Had Elizabeth been able to encounter his eye, she might have seen how well the expression of heartfelt delight, diffused over his face, became him; but, though she could not look, she could listen, and he told her of feelings, which, in proving of what importance she was to him, made his affection every moment more valuable. (*PP* III.16, 406–07)

It is the sort of elaboration or periphrasis that Richardson gave to Pamela as she moved up in the world. There is considerably more detail here about the physical behavior of the two parties to the conversation than in my two prior examples, but the narrator still paraphrases Elizabeth's words as a form of protection; there is a move into the impersonal or passive construction when it comes to Darcy's response ("The happiness" is the subject of the sentence, not Darcy himself, and the verb "be supposed" removes us from Darcy's actual experience to the reader's mental construction), and the narrator yet again concludes by turning our gaze away from the two almost as Elizabeth turns her eyes away from Darcy.

When it comes to the proposal, the narrator of *Mansfield Park* is at least as protective as and perhaps even more strongly personified than its counterparts in the earlier novels. When Edmund tells Fanny about his last conversation with Mary Crawford, and their final separation, the narrator is already invoking (though it is not a proposal) that gesture toward a protective privacy: "How Fanny listened, with what curiosity and concern, what pain and what delight, how the agitation of his voice was watched, and how carefully her own eyes were fixed on any object but himself, may be imagined" (*MP* III.16, 525). We can think of this in terms of a sort of double looking-away, one that echoes the technique of *Pride and Prejudice*: Fanny looks away to protect Edmund from knowing either how attentive she is to his emotional pain or how discrepant her own emotions are from what he imagines them to be; the narrator looks away to protect Fanny from readerly intrusion, or at least to expose her only as much as is strictly necessary (which is to say obliquely, by leaving it up to the reader's imagination even in a conjectural mode).

The "I" of a personified narrator (though still, I think, a narrator without a body) will emerge very strongly in the pages that follow. This is the opening of volume 3, chapter 17:

> Let other pens dwell on guilt and misery. I quit such odious subjects as soon as I can, impatient to restore every body, not greatly in fault themselves, to tolerable comfort, and to have done with all the rest.
>
> My Fanny indeed at this very time, I have the satisfaction of knowing, must have been happy in spite of every thing. She must have been a happy creature in spite of all that she felt or thought she felt, for the distress of those around her. (*MP* III.17, 533)

There is always something proprietary – something of ownership – in the relationship between Austen narrator and Austen heroine, but the possessive pronoun "My" here suggests a specially intense sense of ownership, and the assertion of personal satisfaction – of personal knowledge – is striking. Then, too, that familiar ostentation around the question of what is not specified, what will be left to the reader's imagination, can be discerned in the description of Edmund falling in love with Fanny:

> I purposely abstain from dates on this occasion, that every one may be at liberty to fix their own, aware that the cure of unconquerable passions, and the transfer of unchanging attachments, must vary much as to time in different people.—I only intreat every body to believe that exactly at the time when it was quite natural that it should be so, and not a week earlier, Edmund did cease to care about Miss Crawford, and became as anxious to marry Fanny, as Fanny herself could desire. (*MP* III.17, 544)

And that deferral from authorial specification toward readerly imagining will also characterize the proposal scenes that conclude *Emma* and *Persuasion*.

When Mr. Knightley speaks words of love, Emma is initially silent. His words are completely unexpected though devoutly wished by her, and she has to adjust her answer to suit this very welcome new reality: "She spoke then, on being so entreated.—What did she say?—Just what she ought, of course. A lady always does.—She said enough to show there need not be despair—and to invite him to say more himself" (*E* III.13, 468–69). And the move toward ever-greater stylization and abstraction, the vanishing of specifics under a decorous veil, finds its apex in *Persuasion*'s treatment of the long-awaited engagement between Anne and Captain Wentworth:

> soon words enough had passed between them to decide their direction towards the comparatively quiet and retired gravel-walk, where the power of conversation would make the present hour a blessing indeed; and prepare it for all the immortality which the happiest recollections of their own future lives could bestow. There they exchanged again those feelings and those promises which had once before seemed to secure every thing, but which had been followed by so many, many years of division and estrangement. (*P* II.11, 261)

As in *Mansfield Park*, there is that gesture toward a future of settled, happy, married life, a strange jumping-ahead to enable retrospection; indeed, both distant past and unknown future are curiously more strongly alive here than any real sense of the scene of the present moment. The phrase "the power of conversation would make the present hour a blessing indeed" takes almost as far as it can go the principle that human intimacy needs to be protected from the potentially intrusive or indecorous act of narrative specification, and a neoclassical or sentimental decorum here displaces the aesthetic of realism so often on display elsewhere in Austen's fiction.

CHAPTER 7

Female Economies

There is a tendency to think of the settings of Austen's novels as if they resemble *Downton Abbey* a hundred years earlier: gorgeous, grand country houses, dozens of beautifully dressed couples dancing at balls, carriages and horses and parks and elaborate morning dress. Austen didn't live that kind of a life herself, and many of the characters in her novels are living far more constrained lives in the material sense than the people we usually see in period drama. They aren't inhabiting grand, beautiful, well-heated rooms, they're living in cramped, crowded ones: rooms that are too cold, too hot or otherwise ill-suited to cultivating physical comfort and emotional prosperity. *Mansfield Park* provides the most dramatic contrast between different indoor settings. At Mansfield, Fanny is relegated as a dependent cousin to an attic bedroom (one that might more properly have been given to a servant in this social milieu), and she is able to claim the former schoolroom as her own preserve because of the "deficiency of space and accommodation in her little chamber above" (*MP* I.16, 177). The female Bertram cousins assent because even this larger room is so clearly inferior to their own.

There is no fire in it, at Mrs. Norris' stipulation (remember that this is well before the days of central heating, and that even now large English country houses are often what most Americans would consider deficient in the matter of warmth), and there is a dearth of material comforts, but it is nonetheless Fanny's refuge, not least because of the warmth of childhood memory behind it:

> The room was most dear to her, and she would not have changed its furniture for the handsomest in the house, though what had been originally plain, had suffered all the ill-usage of children—and its greatest elegancies and ornaments were a faded footstool of Julia's work, too ill done for the drawing-room, three transparencies, made in a rage for transparencies, for the three lower panes of one window, where Tintern Abbey held its station between a cave in Italy, and a moonlight lake in Cumberland; a collection of

family profiles thought unworthy of being anywhere else, over the mantel-
piece, and by their side and pinned against the wall, a small sketch of a ship
sent four years ago from the Mediterranean by William, with H. M. S.
Antwerp at the bottom, in letters as tall as the mainmast. (*MP* I.16, 178–79)

A room of one's own is an enormous luxury, of course, something Virginia
Woolf was well aware of when she called it a necessity for a woman writer.
Austen herself never had one on a regular basis, though sharing a bedroom
with her beloved sister, Cassandra, was probably a matter of love as well as
of limited resources in a family with many children and not a great deal of
money.

There is relatively little description of rooms and their insides in
Austen's fiction. My late lamented colleague Karl Kroeber used to tease
the graduate student preceptors of Literature Humanities, when he gave
the instructor lecture on *Pride and Prejudice*, by asking them what the
furniture is like in the room where Darcy proposes to Elizabeth for the first
time. Once they admitted that they didn't remember, Karl would trium-
phantly observe that this was because Austen doesn't specify! But *Mansfield
Park* differs meaningfully from *Pride and Prejudice* in this regard, making
an important point about women's confinement to domestic interiors that
often leave a great deal to be desired. There is comedy in the schoolroom
description, and in the fondness Austen discerns in Fanny for such a
motley collection of furnishings; there is something more of tragedy,
perhaps, or at least a very real threat to well-being, in the physical environ-
ment of Fanny's parents' home at Portsmouth.

Sir Thomas Bertram has sent Fanny home so that she will think twice
about the cost of turning down Henry Crawford's proposal, but her years
at Mansfield Park have eroded Fanny's desensitization to the squalor of
ordinary lower-middle-class life. The sun coming into the parlor is "only a
glare, a stifling, sickly glare, serving but to bring forward stains and dirt that
might otherwise have slept": Fanny's own feelings can be discerned in the
hyperbolic intensity of the language, just as something of Fanny's own
desperate feeling of being trapped colors the pronouncement that follows.

> There was neither health nor gaiety in sun-shine in a town. She sat in a blaze
> of oppressive heat, in a cloud of moving dust; and her eyes could only
> wander from the walls marked by her father's head, to the table cut and
> knotched by her brothers, where stood the tea-board never thoroughly
> cleaned, the cups and saucers wiped in streaks, the milk a mixture of
> motes floating in thin blue, and the bread and butter growing every minute
> more greasy than even Rebecca's hands had first produced it. (*MP*
> III.15, 508)

It is the opposite of luxury: even the milk is contaminated, adulterated (adulterated food was a common problem for city dwellers in eighteenth- and nineteenth-century England, as described most graphically in the first letter in volume two of Tobias Smollett's epistolary novel *Humphry Clinker* (1771)), and the near invisibility of high-class servants in a great house has been superseded by the all-too-present hands of the lowly servant who tends to the Price family's needs.[1] This is the room in which Mr. Price comes across the item in the newspaper about Maria Rushworth's adulter- ous elopement with Henry Crawford and says that if she were his daughter, "I'd give her the rope's end as long as I could stand over her" (*MP* III.15, 509), so that the sordid nature of the physical setting anticipates the brutality of Mr. Price's response to Maria's transgression.

This isn't the only way in which *Mansfield Park* runs scenarios about how women will fare in different socioeconomic and material environ- ments. The novel's opening paragraph is set up as a fairy tale that rapidly devolves into a lesson in inequality. We learn of three sisters and their three very different fates and fortunes as they are determined by marriage:

> About thirty years ago, Miss Maria Ward of Huntington, with only seven thousand pounds, had the good luck to captivate Sir Thomas Bertram, of Mansfield Park, in the county of Northampton, and to be thereby raised to the rank of a baronet's lady, with all the comforts and consequences of an handsome house and large income. All Huntingdon exclaimed on the greatness of the match, and her uncle, the lawyer, himself, allowed her to be at least three thousand pounds short of any equitable claim to it. She had two sisters to be benefited by her elevation; and such of their acquaintance as thought Miss Ward and Miss Frances quite as handsome as Miss Maria, did not scruple to predict their marrying with almost equal advantage. But there certainly are not so many men of large fortune in the world, as there are pretty women to deserve them. (*MP* I.1, 3)

The precision with which the narrator enumerates Maria Ward's fortune isn't just gossipy or incidental. These numbers *matter* in this world: physical attractiveness matters too, but the really important determining factor in a young woman's marriage prospects will almost always be her fortune, and there is clearly a standard calculus around such matters. The uncle's assessment is meant to be honest, humorous and self-deprecating, but its notation in the narrative also produces an effect of irony, calling into question the rationality of a system that evaluates women and their pro- spects with such ruthless numeracy.

The young lady's two sisters are not, as it happens, much elevated by their sister's good fortune. The oldest of the three marries a clergyman called Mr. Norris, a friend of Sir Thomas Bertram who has "scarcely any private fortune" (i.e., only the income he receives by way of his appointments in the church), although Sir Thomas is happily "able to give his friend an income in the living of Mansfield" – an income that we are told is close to a thousand a year, near to the amount that Elinor Dashwood in *Sense and Sensibility* deemed wealth. When Frances marries a naval lieutenant "without education, fortune, or connections," a falling-out ensues, and the novel shows us the very material consequences of that marriage in the wild physical discrepancies and different potentialities that exist in the lives of the children of Mansfield and those of Portsmouth.

Novels can always be thought of as running counterfactual scenarios in some more or less implicit fashion. English literature's most famous signaling of counterfactual alternatives probably comes in the prelude to George Eliot's *Middlemarch* (1871–72), where Eliot invokes the life of Saint Theresa as context for the story of her own protagonist, Dorothea Brooke: "Many Theresas have been born who found for themselves no epic life wherein there was a constant unfolding of far-resonant action; perhaps only a life of mistakes, the offspring of a certain spiritual grandeur ill-matched with the meanness of opportunity; perhaps a tragic failure which found no sacred poet and sank unwept into oblivion."[2] Published in a forum on counterfactual realities in the journal *Representations*, Andrew Miller's essay "Lives Unled in Realist Fiction" offers a striking statement of this aspect of the realist novel:

> To the extent that realism proposes to give us stories about how things really were, a space naturally opens up within that mode to tell us how things might have been, but were not . . . In regularly shadowing forth lives for our characters that we do not see, realism reminds us of the singularity of those lives that we *do* see: it is this life, lived thus, and not other possible lives, formed by other choices, other chances, that the author has decided to represent.[3]

Toward the end of *Mansfield Park*, Austen explicitly signals to counterfactual scenarios in order to underline the arbitrary nature of the fit between any individual woman's fate and her particular capacities:

> Of her two sisters, Mrs. Price very much more resembled Lady Bertram than Mrs. Norris. She was a manager by necessity, without any of Mrs. Norris's inclination for it, or any of her activity. Her disposition was naturally easy and indolent, like Lady Bertram's; and a situation of similar affluence and do-nothing-ness would have been much more suited to her capacity, than the exertions and self-denials of the one, which her imprudent marriage had placed her in. She might have made just as good a woman of consequence as

> Lady Bertram, but Mrs. Norris would have been a more respectable mother
> of nine children, on a small income. (*MP* III.8, 451)

It is a rather extraordinary admission. Mrs. Norris is an unattractive
character, the person whose domination of Fanny causes her undue grief
and whose blind partiality for Maria Bertram is held chiefly accountable for
the distortion and degradation of Maria's values. And yet the narrator is
able to be even-handed in the assessment of her merit, though we should be
aware too of the limits of the meaning of words: "respectable" in particular
is used with a sort of dry reservation and an awareness of the word's root
meaning, certainly not serving as an outright disparagement or detraction
and yet with the sense that when it comes to motherly virtues, "respectable" is setting the bar pretty low.

It is difficult for us now, in the Anglo-American world of the twenty-
first century, to imagine the degree of constraint that governed the
movement outside the home, in the England of Austen's time, of
women who laid claim to any degree of gentility. Working-class
women, at least in the countryside, potentially had more freedom of
movement; wealthy women, especially once they were married, had
access to horses and carriages; but for women like Jane and Cassandra
Austen, not well-enough off to ride horses or have a carriage, winter
especially could impose an almost unimaginable degree of confinement
to the home. Walking solo was deemed off-limits in many contexts (think
of Emma venturing a walk on her own and finding it unpleasant enough
that she co-opts Harriet Smith as her daily walking companion), but in
an age before paved roads and where class decorum prescribed certain
sorts of footwear and prohibited others, muddy country roads would
have in any case rendered walking nearly impossible for many months of
the year. Think of the mean-spirited comments of the Bingley sisters on
Elizabeth Bennet walking about the countryside: "Her hair so untidy, so
blowsy!," comments Caroline Bingley, and her married sister caps it with
the observation, "Yes, and her petticoat; I hope you saw her petticoat, six
inches deep in mud, I am absolutely certain; and the gown which had
been let down to hide it, not doing its office" (*PP* I.8, 39). The sisters
think it shows "an abominable sort of conceited independence, a most
country town indifference to decorum" – what it really shows, we understand, is that Elizabeth Bennet is a pragmatist who will get to her sister's
side by whatever means necessary.

Austen's early unfinished novel "The Watsons" contains another revealing discussion of women and walking. Emma Watson is talking with Lord

Osborne, not himself a gifted conversationalist and here struggling to make appropriate small talk:

> "Have you been walking this morning?"
> "No, my Lord. We thought it too dirty."
> After another pause, "Nothing sets off a neat ancle more than a half-boot; nankin galoshed with black looks very well.—Do not you like half-boots?"
> "Yes—but unless they are so stout as to injure their beauty, they are not fit for country walking.—"
> "Ladies should ride in dirty weather.—Do you ride?"
> "No my Lord."
> "I wonder every lady does not.—A woman never looks better than on horseback.—"
> "But every woman may not have the inclination, or the means."
> "If they knew how much it became them, they would all have the inclination—and I fancy Miss Watson—when once they had the inclination, the means would soon follow."—
> "Your Lordship thinks we always have our own way.—*That* is a point on which ladies and gentlemen have long disagreed.—But without pretending to decide it, I may say that there are some circumstances which even *women* cannot control.—Female economy will do a great deal my Lord, but it cannot turn a small income into a large one."—
> Lord Osborne was silenced. Her manner had been neither sententious nor sarcastic, but there was a something in its mild seriousness, as well as in the words themselves, which made his Lordship think;—and when he addressed her again, it was with a degree of considerate propriety, totally unlike the half-awkward, half-fearless stile of his former remarks. (*LM* 116)

This is a nice little scene in which the heroine makes a serious and thoughtful point about class privilege, and the record of Austen's own letters makes clear how very often the limitations of muddy roads caused significant inconvenience to Austen and her closest female relatives. Austen herself walked whenever it was possible, and there are moments when she chaffs her sister for complaining about the condition of the roads:

> "A very sloppy lane" last Friday!—What an odd sort of country you must be in! I cannot at all understand it! It was just greasy here on Friday, in consequence of the little snow that had fallen in the night.—Perhaps it was <u>cold</u> on Wednesday, yes, I beleive it certainly was—but nothing terrible.—Upon the whole, the Weather for Winter-weather is delightful, the walking excellent. (*JAL* 209)

Anna Lefroy remembered Cassandra and Jane's frequent visits, "& how they walked in wintry weather through the sloppy lane between Steventon & Dean in pattens, usually worn at that time even by Gentlewomen"

(*MJA* 157). (The wearing of pattens, thick wooden-soled overshoes, was increasingly becoming a class marker as nineteenth-century manners imposed more constraints on women's behavior, and the two Austen sisters' habit of winter walking may have been one of the factors that led the more self-consciously genteel Austen relatives to deem Cassandra and Jane old-fashioned and countrified in their manners.)

When the roads were impassable on foot due to dirt and mud, Austen and other women in a similar position were wholly dependent for transportation on the kindness of their more prosperous male friends and relatives. When Austen is eager to visit a newly married Anna before a trip to London the following Wednesday, the visit can only take place on Monday or Tuesday: "if Monday therefore should appear too dirty for walking, & Mr. B.L. [Anna's husband] would be so kind as to come & fetch me to spend some part of the morning with you," Austen writes to Anna, "I should be much obliged to him" (*JAL* 303). And again, Anna is better after feeling very ill early in her pregnancy, and Austen observes of her pregnant niece that "she is quite equal to walking to Chawton, & comes over to us when she can, but the rain & dirt divide us a good deal" (*JAL* 341). The Austen household at Steventon had a donkey carriage reserved for transporting the elderly and ill who were not well enough to walk, but it couldn't be used on very muddy roads. Pregnancy came with other costs as well: "Anna has not a chance of escape; her husband called here the other day, & said she was <u>pretty well</u> but not <u>equal to so long</u> a walk; <u>she must come in</u> her <u>Donkey Carriage.</u>—Poor Animal, she will be worn out before she is thirty.—I am very sorry for her.—Mrs Clement too is in that way again. I am quite tired of so many Children" (*JAL* 351).

Having watched two sisters-in-law suffer through multiple pregnancies that damaged their health and culminated in death, directly or indirectly a result of excessive childbearing, Jane and Cassandra Austen probably found it dispiriting to see pregnancy and childbirth encroach on the health of a beloved niece. It is easy to romanticize marriage or to take at face value the notion that someone like Jane Austen, in an ideal world, would have had a marriage like Elizabeth Bennet's or Anne Elliot's, but maternal mortality was such that marriage in this era, for women of all social classes, was more likely to hurt than help the health of the wife (think of Charlotte Brontë, who survived longer than her siblings but died toward the end of her first pregnancy in her late thirties, or of Mary Wollstonecraft, who died of puerperal fever following the birth of her second daughter). Neither are Austen's comments on childbirth in the letters particularly reassuring, though there is an early playful one that contrasts two of the sisters-in-law and their situation (satirical and frivolous as the observation may be, one suspects that there might have been some underlying truth to it):

> Mary does not manage matters in such a way as to make me want to lay in myself. She is not tidy enough in her appearance; she has no dressing-gown to sit up in; her curtains are all too thin, and things are not in that comfort and style about her which are necessary to make such a situation an enviable one. Elizabeth was really a pretty object with her nice clean cap put on so tidily and her dress so uniformly white and orderly. (*JAL* 25)

The wealthier women in Austen's novels often use their ill health to manipulate others and domineer over them: think of Mrs. Ferrars in *Sense and Sensibility*, or of Lady Catherine de Bourgh's conviction that her daughter's delicate health is a mark of distinction. In her letters as well as in her fiction, Austen amuses herself by contemplating the manipulative potential of a good health problem, commenting for instance in an 1813 letter on visitor Mrs. Bridges, "They have been all the summer at Ramsgate, for <u>her</u> health, she is a poor Honey—the sort of woman who gives me the idea of being determined never to be well–& who likes her spasms & nervousness & the consequence they give her, better than anything else" (*JAL* 240). Ramsgate was one of the new spa towns that had sprung up during the years of the cultivation of sensibility by way of an associated industry of remedies and treatment regimens; Austen's last unfinished fiction, *Sanditon*, is set in a town whose proprietors want it to become a resort of this nature, and it is preoccupied with the distortions of health experienced by a set of self-proclaimed invalids whose bodies fall along the spectrum from self-deprivation to self-indulgence. The ailing Parker siblings represent both extremes of that spectrum: Arthur Parker depends heavily on wine and large quantities of butter to bolster his already large frame (*LM* 196, 198), whereas sisters Diana and Susan Parker hew to a more extreme discipline of self-punishment. Diana's letter to her brother Mr. Parker about their sister Susan explains that in order to cure her headache, she has had three teeth drawn, something that elicits Charlotte's horror: "Three teeth drawn at once!—frightful!" (*LM* 164–65). For the Parker sisters, though, such mortifications of the flesh offer a powerful means of self-expression and self-aggrandizement.

Austen's letters provide regular glimpses of the woes of contemporary dentistry. (Even in our own time, I find that there is nothing so likely to make me feel that I am embodied in the decaying flesh of a Francis Bacon subject than having my teeth cleaned by a heavy-handed hygienist.) A trip to London was often the occasion for seeing the dentist (Harriet's trip to

London in *Emma* would provide a fictional analog), and Austen wrote of one such visit:

> The poor Girls & their Teeth!—I have not mentioned them yet, but we were a whole hour at Spence's, & Lizzy's were filed & lamented over again & poor Marianne had two taken out after all, the two just beyond the Eye teeth, to make room for those in front.—When her doom was fixed, Fanny Lizzy & I walked into the next room, where we heard each of the two sharp hasty Screams.—Fanny's teeth were cleaned too–& pretty as they are, Spence found something to do to them, putting in gold & talking gravely—& making a considerable point of seeing her again before winter; . . . The little girls teeth I can suppose in a critical state, but I think he must be a Lover of Teeth & Money & Mischeif to parade about Fannys. (*JAL* 233)

A very bad set of teeth could materially affect the fate and fortunes of a young woman hoping to be married, and the loss of teeth (or the possession of unsightly teeth) was not just physically painful but potentially consequential in other domains of life. An Austen cousin commented of Jane's mother in middle age that she had "lost several fore-teeth which makes her look old" (*FR* 64), and there is a very memorable scene, in novelist Elizabeth Jane Howard's multi-novel chronicle of the Cazalet family, in which Cazalet daughter Louise comes home and finds her beautiful mother Villy "on the sofa in the drawing room, crying, something that she had never seen before in her life":

> She had rushed to the sofa, knelt by it, asked her again and again what was the matter. Her mother took her hands away from her face, and Louise saw that it was all puffy and bruised and she had wet, frightened eyes. 'They've taken out all my teeth,' she said. She touched the sides of her face and began to cry again.[4]

There is nothing quite so graphic as that in Austen, but the threat of decay and decline – in mouth, in body – was very much present, and Austen's own health took a sharp decline in her late thirties. She was dead at forty-one of an illness that the medicine of her own time had no power to diagnose or treat but that has been speculatively identified more recently as Addison's disease.

It is easy even for a marriage skeptic to find the best marriages in Austen's novels attractive, but the reality of the marriage possibilities available to Austen and her female peer group was much less rosy. This does come through to some extent in the novels, despite their happy endings, but the letters reveal a more dismal realm of possibility. Cassandra was engaged to be married, but her fiancé died overseas, and she never formed another serious attachment. Austen in her teens seems to have fallen for a young man called

Tom Lefroy, the nephew of her good friend Mrs. Lefroy, but he was not in a financial position to make her an offer, and when she later received a marriage proposal from the brother of two close female friends, she accepted it initially and then retracted that acceptance the next morning, causing both families a certain degree of pain. Part of the trouble was that for women who came from a genteel social class but had relatively scanty financial resources, there were truly no good options outside marriage: Charlotte Lucas' choice to marry Mr. Collins in preference to remaining an unmarried daughter in the paternal home is the sort of opportunity many real women in this time would have welcomed.

Austen's fiction *The Watsons*, which some critics have suggested breaks off because Austen realized that its vision of women's prospects was unredeemably bleak, includes one of the most up-front treatments of the marriage calculus. Our female protagonist, Emma Watson, has been brought up by an aunt who until recently has been comparatively well-off but has now sacrificed her future by marrying a fortune hunter. She can no longer take care of Emma or promise her any kind of inheritance, and when Emma returns to her father's house, her older sisters are more in touch than she is with the dire financial and social realities of their situation. In the passage that follows, Austen seems to be at once endorsing an attractive character's sentiments and ironizing them by setting them in apposition to underlying economic and social realities. Emma, embarrassed by the brazenness of her sister's search for a husband, reproaches her sister for being "so bent on marriage": "Poverty is a great evil," she tells her sister, "but to a woman of education and feeling it ought not, it cannot be the greatest.—I would rather be teacher at a school (and I can think of nothing worse) than marry a man I did not like" (*LM* 83). Her sister's response has a certain blunt authority: "I would rather do any thing than be teacher at a school— ... *I* have been at school, Emma, and know what a life they lead; *you* never have."

The trouble is that their father's establishment depends on his remaining alive and drawing his income as a clergyman, but his health is failing, and after his death the daughters will be homeless. Their insensitive brother rubs in how bereft Emma has become now that her aunt has been conned out of her fortune:

> "I did not mean to make you cry—" said Robert rather softened—and after a short silence, by way of changing the subject, he added—"I am just come from my father's room, he seems very indifferent. It will be a sad break-up when he dies. Pity, you can none of you get married!—You must come to Croydon as well as the rest, and see what you can do there.—I believe if

Margaret had had a thousand or fifteen hundred pounds, there was a young
man who would have thought of her." (*LM* 124)

It is a savage indictment of the ways this world limits women's prospects
based on their financial assets.

Claire Tomalin's biography of the novelist emphasizes a ten-year period
of silence: by her mid-twenties, Austen had drafted three very promising
novels, but it was only ten years later, in the summer of 1809 and at the age
of thirty-five, that she would find herself in a position to return to the
working patterns and productivity of her early twenties (169–70). The
most significant factor is likely to have been the Austen daughters' expul-
sion from their lifelong home following their father's decision to resign his
position and cede the living at Steventon to Jane Austen's brother James,
also a clergyman, with the Austen parents and daughters moving to a much
narrower life in Bath. It was a sort of exile, one that came with tedious and
extensive social obligations and a much less clear sense of identity and
community than life at the vicarage had facilitated, and Anne Elliot's
aversion to the prospect of life at Bath probably owes something to
Austen's own experience.

After Jane Austen died, Cassandra cut out passages from the letters that
reflected negatively on family members or complained too much about
their situation, destroying many letters in their entirety, but a few acerbic
comments did escape her censorship. Here Austen resists pressure to leave
for her niece Anna, James' daughter, one of her own most precious
possessions: "You are very kind in planning presents for me to make, &
my Mother has shewn me exactly the same attention—but as I do not
chuse to have Generosity dictated to me, I shall not resolve on giving my
Cabinet to Anna till the first thought of it has been my own" (*JAL* 74).
Many of the family's possessions were sold at auction, mostly at a disadvantage: "Mr Bent seems <u>bent</u> on being very detestable," Austen writes
some months later, "for he values the books at only £70. The whole World
is in a conspiracy to enrich one part of our family at the expence of
another" (*JAL* 92).

The individual story of dispossession that the Austen daughters experienced, a story that finds echoes in the opening of *Sense and Sensibility* as
well as in *Pride and Prejudice*, was in many respects the consequence of
larger social trends that had been operating for half a century or more.
Ruth Perry has chronicled the sociological underpinnings of this disposs-
session, telling the story of a major restructuring of kinship ties over the
course of the long eighteenth century that "affected what it meant to be a

daughter, a sister, an aunt, an uncle, a son, or a brother": the replacement of what in the earlier time had been a kinship system based on blood with a conjugal kinship system, one where a woman married into her husband's family rather than retaining an identity based on affiliation to her own father's line.[5] Perry argues that this transition (it is part of the movement from a status-based society to a class-based one) resulted in a massive psychological (and sometimes also legal) disinheritance of daughters at the expense of sons. Perhaps the worst irony of the dispossession was that it would be repeated in every generation. James Austen's family had displaced his father's family from the parsonage, but in due time illness and death would lead to James being replaced by his brother Henry as incumbent of the living at Steventon, and one of James' daughters wrote with chagrin of this succession: "[Henry] was always very affectionate in manner to us, and paid my mother every due attention, but his own spirits he could <u>not</u> repress, and it is not pleasant to <u>witness</u> the elation of your successor in gaining what <u>you</u> have lost" (*FR* 262–63).

The opening paragraph of chapter 7 of *Pride and Prejudice* lays out the financial situation facing the Bennet family: "Mr. Bennet's property consisted almost entirely in an estate of two thousand a year, which, unfortunately for his daughters, was entailed in default of heirs male, on a distant relation; and their mother's fortune, though ample for her situation in life, could but ill supply the deficiency of his" (*PP* I.7, 31). One reason the Bennets have five children is presumably that they continued to try for a male heir, since that heir could unite with the current possessor of the property to "break" an entail. Edward Gibbon was forced to do this by his spendthrift father, though it was far from being to his own financial advantage, and such entails were really intended not just to keep estates from being divided but to protect sons' interests from bad decision-making on the part of irresponsible fathers.

We may think of looks as one of the important determining features of women's marriage prospects, and certainly they were not negligible (a great beauty might transcend economic strictures, especially at the higher end of the social spectrum, where men were more likely to be in a position to marry to please themselves), but in this social milieu a young woman's fortune had a much more obvious and direct effect on her marriageability than her physical attractiveness as such. Mr. Collins crudely expresses what was surely a widespread social consensus when he tells Elizabeth Bennet, after she has refused his proposal of marriage, that he can't accept her negative answer:

"It does not appear to me that my hand is unworthy your acceptance, or that the establishment I can offer would be any other than highly desirable. My situation in life, my connections with the family of De Bourgh, and my relationship to your own, are circumstances highly in my favour; and you should take it into farther consideration that in spite of your manifold attractions, it is by no means certain that another offer of marriage may ever be made you. Your portion is unhappily so small that it will in all likelihood undo the effects of your loveliness and amiable perfections." (*PP* I.19, 121–22)

The creepiness of Mr. Collins' hyperbolic complimenting here only underlines the weakness of the position in which a young woman like Elizabeth Bennet finds herself. Her less personally attractive friend Charlotte Lucas can't afford this kind of scruple – Mr. Collins, set on changing his single status before he returns home and undaunted by the fact that he has just proposed to another woman, will find a happier answer at Lucas Lodge than he does at Longbourn. The narrator's summing-up comment on Charlotte's acceptance of his proposal is sharply ironic: "The stupidity with which he was favoured by nature, must guard his courtship from any charm that could make a woman wish for its continuance; and Miss Lucas, who accepted him solely from the pure and disinterested desire of an establishment, cared not how soon that establishment were gained" (*PP* I.22, 137).

The concreteness of the sense everyone in this world has of money in relation to marriageability (think of that passage about the Ward sisters in the opening of *Mansfield Park*) calls to mind for me the ways that U.S. college advisors can tell a graduating senior with near certainty, on the basis of grade point average and LSAT scores, which law schools will admit her. Consider the discussion Elizabeth and Jane Bennet have with their father after getting the news from their uncle that Wickham will marry Lydia after all, on terms that his letter enumerates: her share of her mother's fortune will be settled on her (that's a thousand pounds, which should produce an annual income of fifty pounds, assuming a five percent return), in addition to an annual allowance from her father of a hundred pounds (i.e., the income on another two thousand pounds). Mr. Bennet is relieved but worried, as it's clear to him that this only scratches the surface of what must have been done for the young couple: "there are two things that I want very much to know," he says mournfully: "–one is, how much money your uncle has laid down, to bring it about; and the other, how am I ever to pay him" (*PP* III.7, 335). The girls are insufficiently knowledgeable to have worldly contexts for this sort of financial transaction, but their father goes on to tell them that he thinks Wickham's "a fool, if he takes [Lydia] with a farthing less than ten thousand pounds" (a farthing is just a very small unit of coinage, a quarter of a penny). A lump sum on that scale, prudently invested, could be expected in this setting to produce an annual income of five hundred pounds; men were mostly supposed to consolidate and improve their social and economic position by marriage, not to take on deadweight.

This is why Mr. Knightley thinks Robert Martin could do better than Harriet Smith: for the yeoman-farmer class as well as for the class of clergymen and professionals, marriage is how wealth is increased and passed on to the next generation, with assets passing from the daughter's birth family to the family she marries into. Given this underlying financial reality, young women needed to be extremely prudent in their choices. A woman who married without the necessary backing would either become an ongoing drain on her father's income, with the cost of a married daughter's separate establishment greatly outweighing the sort of minor maintenance or "pin money" that was commonly allocated to unmarried daughters who lived at home, or else risked falling into absolute indigence.

For this reason and others, young women with pretensions to gentility were expected to act with significant decorum and self-restraint. This kind of norm could become self-defeating. Elizabeth Bennet considers it an advantage that her sister Jane "united with great strength of feeling, a composure of temper and a uniform cheerfulness of manner, which would guard her from the suspicions of the impertinent" (*PP* I.6, 23), but Charlotte Lucas points out that such self-concealment, even if it is conducive to self-protection, may also be tactically disadvantageous: "If a woman conceals her affection with the same skill from the object of it, she may lose the opportunity of fixing him; and it will then be but poor consolation to believe the world equally in the dark," she says. "In nine cases out of ten, a woman had better shew *more* affection than she feels" (*PP* I.6, 24).

That said, naked self-interest is even more unattractive in women than in men, and Austen's novels don't hesitate to condemn behavior that is too clearly driven by mercenary motives, as in the narrative summing-up of Lucy Steele's triumph in the form of marriage to Robert Ferrars:

> The whole of Lucy's behaviour in the affair, and the prosperity which crowned it, therefore, may be held forth as a most encouraging instance of what an earnest, an unceasing attention to self-interest, however its progress may be apparently obstructed, will do in securing every

advantage of fortune, with no other sacrifice than that of time and conscience. (*SS* III.14, 426)

The character of Mrs. Clay provides a close parallel in *Persuasion*, but though the sacrifice of time and conscience in such goals is roundly condemned, it is hardly surprising that women should fall back on this sort of behavior in a world that gives them so few other options.

There are two sets of letters from late in Austen's life that are more revealing than most of the others. One set gives advice to her niece Anna about novel-writing; the other is a fascinating and intimate sequence of letters Austen sent to her niece Fanny in the months when she was deciding who to marry. A highly eligible suitor had presented himself; Fanny was initially very much taken with him, but lost enthusiasm shortly thereafter. Austen's first piece of advice involves recommending to her niece that she fall "in love with him again":

> There <u>are</u> such beings in the World perhaps, one in a Thousand, as the Creature You & I should think perfection, where Grace & Spirit are united to Worth, where the Manners are equal to the Heart & Understanding, but such a person may not come in your way, or if he does, he may not be the eldest son of a Man of Fortune, the Brother of your particular friend, & belonging to your own County. (*JAL* 292)

It is a very practical laying out of the young man's advantages, but Austen then goes on to qualify her enthusiasm: "And now, my dear Fanny, having written so much on one side of the question, I shall turn round & entreat you not to commit yourself farther, & not to think of accepting him unless you really do like him. Anything is to be preferred or endured rather than marrying without Affection; and if his deficiencies of Manner &c &c strike you more than all his good qualities, if you continue to think strongly of them, give him up at once" (*JAL* 292–93). He will be disappointed for a time, she adds, "but it is no creed of mine, as you must be well aware, that such sort of Disappointments kill anybody" (*JAL* 293).

The letters that follow reveal a certain degree of anxiety on Austen's part that Fanny is giving too much credit to her aunt's advice: "Your own feelings & none but your own, should determine such an important point," she writes (*JAL* 298). Especially the risk of entering into a bad marriage is so great that Fanny shouldn't do it unless "[her] own Sentiments prompt it" – "You will think me perverse perhaps," Austen adds; "in my last letter I was urging everything in his favour, & now I am inclining the other way" (*JAL* 298). Even more telling, perhaps, is the playful comment she makes elsewhere, as they continue to consider marital possibilities: "Oh! What a loss it will be, when you are married. You are too agreeable in your single state, too agreeable as a Neice. I shall hate you when your delicious play of Mind is all settled down into conjugal & maternal affections" (*JAL* 343).

None of Austen's protagonists would enter into marriage lightly, but they are mostly favorably inclined toward marriage as a state, with the striking exception of Emma Woodhouse. One of the funniest conversations in *Emma* takes place between Emma and Harriet relatively early on. The comedy comes at Emma's expense mostly, I think, highlighting both her own lack of self-awareness and Harriet's obtuse failure of imagination, although the irony is also directed against a system where such things can be so pervasively thought, not just by Harriet but by others who might not be so naïve as to articulate it but who have bought in equally strongly to the underlying ideology. Marriage is on both young women's minds because of Mr. Elton's recent engagement, and Harriet says to Emma, "I do so wonder, Miss Woodhouse, that you should not be married, or going to be married! So charming as you are!" (*E* I.10, 90). Emma's response is characteristically sharp: "My being charming, Harriet, is not quite enough to induce me to marry; I must find other people charming—one other person at least. And I am not only, not going to be married, at present, but have very little intention of marrying at all." It would need to be someone very superior, Emma continues: "I cannot really change for the better. If I were to marry, I must expect to repent it." (Austen invites us to contemplate Emma's woeful misunderstanding of what marriage really can and should be, a true partnership in which the whole is more than the sum of the two individual parts; at this point in her development, she can only understand marriage in narrow terms of social status.)

Emma goes on to elaborate further on the theme:

> "I have none of the usual inducements of women to marry. Were I to fall in love, indeed, it would be a different thing! But I never have been in love; it is not my way, or my nature; and I do not think I ever shall. And, without love, I am sure I should be a fool to change such a situation as mine. Fortune I do not want; employment I do not want; consequence I do not want: I believe few married women are half as much mistress of their husband's house, as I am of Hartfield; and never, never could I expect to be so truly beloved and important; so always first and always right in any man's eyes as I am in my father's." (*E* I.10, 90–91)

It is another comical misunderstanding, of course, to believe that to be always right in the other person's eyes is one of the best rewards of marriage. Harriet's response is again comically and obtusely on point: "But then, to be an old maid at last, like Miss Bates!"

The novel does indeed give Emma some painful lessons in the limits of her single status, as well as in the limitations of having her behavior remain impervious to criticism. When Mrs. Elton enters the social world of Highbury, she will take social precedence over Emma as a married woman, and she is not the person to cede such an advantage. When she leads the way at the ball later in the novel, it deals a blow to Emma's conviction that the single life suits her best: "Emma must submit to stand second to Mrs. Elton, though she had always considered the ball as peculiarly for her. It was almost enough to make her think of marrying" (*E* III.2, 352). Remember, too, that Emma with all her wealth and privilege has never seen the sea (*E* I.12, 108).

There was a good deal of attention in this period to the difficulties that faced a woman whose husband proved an irresponsible guardian (married women were not legally entitled to own and control property in their own right until Parliament passed the Married Women's Property Act in 1882) or a bad shepherd of the family finances. Wollstonecraft's writing twines closely around this question, indicting bad husbands and fathers for not doing a better job taking care of women who were prevented by society from taking care of themselves. We don't know to what extent Austen was familiar with Wollstonecraft's writings, but such topics were of great concern in the larger social milieu as well, and questions about dispossession, parental negligence and female dependence permeate all of Austen's fiction.

Austen's most direct treatment of women's vulnerability after marriage comes by way of the story of Mrs. Smith, Anne Elliot's old school friend, in the second half of *Persuasion*. This is the novel's description of Mrs. Smith's situation:

> She was a widow, and poor. Her husband had been extravagant; and at his death, about two years before, had left his affairs dreadfully involved. She had had difficulties of every sort to contend with, and in addition to these distresses, had been afflicted with a severe rheumatic fever, which finally settling in her legs, had made her for the present a cripple. She had come to Bath on that account, and was now in lodgings near the hot-baths, living in a very humble way, unable even to afford herself the comfort of a servant, and of course almost excluded from society. (*P* II.5, 166)

The scenario is highly reminiscent of what is almost a primal scene of trauma involving spousal neglect and abuse in the novels of the 1790s and beyond (Wollstonecraft's novel *Maria, or The Wrongs of Woman*, published posthumously in 1798, provides a powerful example). What may be most shocking about the novelist's representation of Mrs. Smith is that it is only once she is positively assured that Anne isn't going to marry William Elliot that Mrs. Smith uncovers the man's vicious character to her friend (*P* II.9, 215). That suggests the depth of the widespread conviction (Mrs. Smith certainly shares it) that a young woman with the opportunity to make an advantageous marriage will place that above almost every other factor of loyalty, love and friendship to her own sex.

Around the edges of Austen's fiction, there are other bleak depictions of women's situation and fortunes. There is an ongoing conversation in the early fiction *Catharine, or the Bower* concerning the pretty but impoverished young women "equipped" for the East Indies with the goal of finding husbands among the upwardly mobile Englishmen who worked for the East India Company (Austen's aunt Philadelphia experienced something very like this fate). *Catharine* depicts a sort of patronage relationship between benefactor Lady Halifax and her niece and dependent Miss Wynne, and part of the point here is to highlight the discrepancy of fortunes between families of first cousins, something Austen knew very well from personal experience. Miss Wynne is one of four children of a clergyman who has given them all a good education but not endowed them with material wealth to speak of, and all of the children have depended on the patronage of relatives to make their way in the world. Our likeable protagonist Catharine's oblivious friend tells her happily that another relative "sent the eldest Girl to India entirely at his own Expence, where they say she is most nobly married and the happiest Creature in the World" (*J* 254); one son was put into the army and the other sent to a school in Wales, while the younger daughter has been taken in by Lady Halifax. All of them, says Catherine's friend, echoing the thoughtless cant of charity, are "the luckiest Creatures in the World," although Catharine notes that it is only those "who have themselves conferred an obligation on them" who call it so: "do you call it lucky, for a Girl of Genius and Feeling to be sent in quest of a Husband to Bengal, to be married there to a Man of whose Disposition she has no opportunity of judging till her Judgement is of no use to her, who may be a Tyrant, or a Fool or both for what she knows to the Contrary. Do you call *that* fortunate?" (*J* 256). "I know nothing of all that," Miss Stanley replies;

> "I only know that it was extremely good in Sir George to fit her out and pay for her Passage, and that she would not have found Many who would have done the same."
>
> "I wish she had not found *one*, said Kitty with great Eagerness, she might then have remained in England and been happy."

"Well, I cannot conceive the hardship of going out in a very agreeable Manner with two or three sweet Girls for Companions, having a delightful voyage to Bengal or Barbadoes or wherever it is, and being married soon after one's arrival to a very charming Man immensely rich—. I see no hardship in all that."

"Your representation of the Affair, said Kitty laughing, certainly gives a very different idea of it from Mine. But supposing all this to be true, still, as it was by no means certain that she would be so fortunate either in her voyage, her Companions, or her husband; in being obliged to run the risk of their proving very different, she undoubtedly experienced a great hardship—. Besides, to a Girl of any Delicacy, the voyage in itself, since the object of it is so universally known, is a punishment that needs no other to make it very severe."

"I do not see that at all. She is not the first Girl who has gone to the East Indies for a Husband, and I declare I should think it very good fun if I were as poor."

"I beleive you would think very differently <u>then</u>. But at least you will not defend her Sister's situation? Dependant even for her Cloathes on the bounty of others, who of course do not pity her, as by your own account, they consider her as very fortunate."

"You are extremely nice upon my word; Lady Halifax is a delightful Woman, and one of the sweetest tempered Creatures in the World[.]"
(J 256–57)

The published fiction tends to be less explicit about this kind of injustice, although it pops through in places like the opening sequence of *Sense and Sensibility*, the picture of Fanny's humiliating dependency in *Mansfield Park* and the hazards Jane Fairfax faces in *Emma*; the sense of tragedy only narrowly averted hovers over several of Austen's endings.

Biographer Claire Tomalin says of Austen's life that it is "not an easy story to investigate" (6). The Austen family experienced a series of major upheavals in the last years of the eighteenth century, changes and traumas (the word is not too strong) that often can only be guessed at: "Some can be glimpsed through Jane's letters," Tomalin notes, "most not at all. Only twenty-eight letters exist for the five years 1796 to 1801, and none at all for the very important year of 1797, because Cassandra took particular care to destroy personal family material" (124). The letters we have, then, Tomalin emphasizes, "are an edited and contrived version" of the life: one that excises almost everything of strong feeling, leaving only the minutiae of daily life with which one might fill up a letter to an absent dear one. Many of these details are poignant in their terribly small scale, and in the vivid sense they convey of the narrowness (financial, geographical) of the Austen sisters' lives during these years.

There is an ongoing conversation, for instance, about the purchase of materials to make dresses – this is partly because whichever sister was in town would be commissioned to make purchases for the other sister as well – that reminds us that in these years before the mass production of clothing, one new dress a year might be considered an extravagance, and dresses were worn by women like Jane and Cassandra Austen until they were about to disintegrate past respectability. "I gave 2s/3d a yard for my flannel, & I fancy it is not very good," Austen writes to Cassandra in their youth; "but it is so disgraceful & contemptible an article in itself, that its' being comparatively good or bad is of little importance" (*JAL* 17). This is the sort of hint on the basis of which we might suspect that Marianne Dashwood's youthful distaste for flannel waistcoats may have been Austen's joke at her own expense.

Not long after, Austen urges Cassandra to "meditate the purchase of a new muslin Gown": "I am determined to buy a handsome one whenever I can," Austen adds, "& I am so tired & ashamed of half my present stock that I even blush at the sight of the wardrobe which contains them.—But I will not be much longer libeled by the possession of my coarse spot, I shall turn it into a petticoat very soon" (*JAL* 31). The "coarse spot" is probably not a stain but a pattern, with the coarseness referring either to the texture of the material or to the large size and scale of the spots, but the letter shows in passing the frugality of life for women of slender means during this period, the importance of their small economies and the all-pervasive limitations on action even down to minute expenditures. On the topic of repurposing from outerwear to underwear, the process could sometimes be hastened in the case of garments one had become tired of, as when Austen writes in 1809 from Bath that she "mean[s] to wear out my spotted Muslin before I go.—You will exclaim at this—but mine really has signs of feebleness, which with a little care may come to something" (*JAL* 173). It is rather the voice of the early satires – Lady Susan has something of this unscrupulous briskness.

Elsewhere Austen asks Cassandra to send their father "an account of your Washing & Letter expences &c, he will send You a draft for the amount of it, as well as for your next quarter, & for Edward's Rent.–If you don't buy a muslin Gown now on the strength of this Money, & Frank's promotion," she adds, "I shall never forgive You" (*JAL* 33). The extravagance is more fictional than real, and there is a constant running tally taking place in the mind of Austen and her closest peers of even the tiniest costs – including, of course, the cost of postage (see Chapter 1, "Letters"). Jokingly, in a letter to Martha Lloyd (the friend closest to the two sisters – she ultimately married

their widowed brother Frank when he was in his sixties), Austen writes:
"I did <u>not</u> receive your note yesterday till after Charlotte had left Deane, or
I would have sent my answer by her, instead of being the means, as I now
must be, of lessing the Elegance of your new Dress for the Hurstbourn Ball
by the value of 3d.—" (*JAL* 60). The joke being that a few pennies spent on
postage (paid by the recipient, as always during this period, unless a parlia-
mentary frank exempted the letter from charges) would have to come off the
price of the new dress.

   Plans to get something new were shared and relished by the Austen
sisters and their friends. Here is another one of those moments (they
are often the occasion for playfulness, and is hard to tell how much the
mock-sensibility concerning poverty is humorous or real – the joke
isn't funny if there isn't some truth to it). "How is your blue gown?"
writes Austen to Cassandra. "—Mine is all to peices.—I think there
must have been something wrong in the dye, for in places it divided
with a Touch.—There was four shillings thrown away;–to be added to
my subjects of never failing regret" (*JAL* 149). Even more difficult was
the fact that propriety rendered it necessary, on the death of family
members, to adopt mourning garb, a challenge to those living within
strict financial limits.

   The ways people of means thoughtlessly (or in some cases maliciously)
exert dominion over those less well-off than they are is one of Austen's
great topics from her earliest years of writing. Think, for instance, of this
passage from one of the "collection of letters" Austen included in *Volume
the Second*, with the title "From A Young Lady in distress'd Circumstances
to her freind" (*J* 197–98). The letter-writer, Maria Williams, examines her
indebtedness to Lady Greville, considering especially the ways her social
superior makes Maria feel her own inferiority: when Lady Greville picks
Maria up in the coach and allows her to "sit forwards" (i.e., facing in the
direction of travel), Maria observes that it "is a favour about which I am
very indifferent especially as I know it is considered as conferring a great
obligation on me" (*J* 198). A compliment from Lady Greville about Maria's
new gown has a sting in its tail, as she also tells the young woman that it is
"quite a needless peice of expence":

> Why could not you have worn your old striped one? It is not my way to find
> fault with people because they are poor, for I always think that they are more
> to be despised and pitied than blamed for it, especially if they cannot help it,
> but at the same time I must say that in my opinion your old striped Gown
> would have been quite fine enough for its wearer—for to tell you the truth
> (I always speak my mind) I am very much afraid that one half of the people

in the room will not know whether you have a Gown on or not—But I suppose you intend to make your fortune tonight—: Well, the sooner the better; and I wish you success. (*J* 198)

Austen's sympathies are usually with those who are condescended to, lectured and disrespected. At one point in *Mansfield Park*, when Fanny is invited to visit the Parsonage as a dinner guest, the officious Mrs. Norris tells her not to put herself forward as if she were one of her cousins: "Remember, wherever you are," she tells Fanny, "you must be the lowest and last" (*MP* II.5, 258). This is Austen's surely deliberately satirical echo of the famous passage in Matthew 19.30 – "But many that are first shall be last; and the last shall be first" – and Mrs. Norris, clergyman's widow notwithstanding, seems to have no ear for her own distortion of the Christian precept.

Another emotionally fraught form of felt inferiority involved relationships with siblings whose marriages and other affiliations had rendered class difference newly a factor. There is a very beautiful passage about fraternal love in *Mansfield Park* in which the narrator emphasizes the power of spending a childhood together and being able to reminisce about it together in later years:

> An advantage this, a strengthener of love, in which even the conjugal tie is beneath the fraternal. Children of the same family, the same blood, with the same first associations and habits, have some means of enjoyment in their power, which no subsequent connections can supply; and it must be by a long and unnatural estrangement, by a divorce which no subsequent connection can justify, if such precious remains of the earliest attachments are ever entirely outlived. Too often, alas! It is so.—Fraternal love, sometimes almost everything, is at others worse than nothing. (*MP* II.6, 274)

It is very likely that Cassandra meant to excise from Austen's letters all negative reflections on brothers and their wives, but hints of discord slip through here and there. Austen writes thus, for instance, of one visit from her brother James: "I am sorry & angry that his Visits should not give one more pleasure; the company of so good & so clever a Man ought to be gratifying in itself;—but his Chat seems all forced, his Opinions on many points too much copied from his Wife's, & his time here is spent I think in walking about the House & banging the Doors, or ringing the Bell for a glass of Water" (*JAL* 126).

Elsewhere Austen jokes about being in social demand and much hosted by others during the early years of exile in Bath: with this degree of hospitality, she adds, "Our Tea & sugar will last a great while.—I think we are just the kind of people & party to be treated about among our relations;—we cannot be supposed to be very rich" (*JAL* 105). And at her brother Edward's grand house at Godmersham Park (he had been adopted into a wealthier branch of the family), there was often some feeling of being a poor relation, or at least a keen sense of the discrepancies between the way of life here and at home: "Rostock Market makes one's mouth water, our cheapest Butcher's meat is double the price of theirs;—nothing under 9d all this Summer, & I beleive on recollection nothing under 10d.—Bread has sunk & is likely to sink more, which we hope may make Meat sink too. But I have no occasion to think of the price of Bread or of Meat where I am now [at Godmersham Park];—let me shake off vulgar cares & conform to the happy indifference of East Kent wealth" (*JAL* 239).

There are only tiny glimpses in the letters of an Austen emotionally vulnerable to love or dreams of marriage of herself. The tone of high excitement in the young flirtatious letter that mentions Tom Lefroy is anomalous – "At length the Day is come on which I am to flirt my last with Tom Lefroy, & when you receive this it will be over—My tears flow as I write, at the melancholy idea" (*JAL* 4) – Tomalin suggests that this letter must have survived Cassandra's purging only by an oversight. One of the difficult things about love in that sort of situation is that it would have been difficult ever to learn anything more about what happened to the person afterward; Tom's aunt Mrs. Lefroy, a great friend of Austen's when she was a teenager, would visit the Austen household at Steventon toward the end of the same year, and Austen comments with what is surely frustration that "of her nephew she said nothing at all, and of her friend very little": "She did not once mention the name of the former to me, and I was too proud to make any enquiries; but on my father's afterwards asking where he was, I learnt that he was gone back to London in his way to Ireland, where he is called to the Bar and means to practice" (*JAL* 19). And that was that.

There is a constant awareness – it comes through especially strongly in *Emma* – of the plight of older penniless women in a society that has so little value for them. In her letters, Austen now and then expresses sympathy for a woman in this sort of situation. When a Miss Murden visits, Austen comments that "at her age perhaps one may be as friendless oneself, & in similar circumstances quite as captious" (*JAL* 168). When Austen reached her thirties, though, she found that era of life to have its compensations. Here she describes a sharp moment of déjà vu at a ball: "It was the same room in which we danced 15 years ago!—I thought it all over—& in spite of the shame of being so much older, felt with Thankfulness that I was quite as happy now as then" (*JAL* 163). Later on she describes a Miss Lee as being "at an age of reason, ten years older than myself at least," adding: "By the bye, as I must leave off being young, I find many Douceurs in being a sort of Chaperon for I am put on the Sofa near the Fire & can drink as much wine as I like" (*JAL* 261). This is in contrast to the physical, intellectual and emotional demands that being a wife and mother put on the women she knew, not least because of the inexorable physical demands of successive pregnancies.

Especially striking is Austen's description of having greatly enjoyed a visit from her brother and yet being "not sorry when Friday came":

> It had been a busy week, & I wanted a few days quiet, & exemption from the Thought & contrivances which any sort of company gives.—I often wonder how you can find time for what you do, in addition to the care of the House;—And how good Mrs West cd have written such Books & collected so many hard words, with all her family cares, is still more a matter of astonishment! Composition seems to me Impossible, with a head full of Joints of Mutton & doses of rhubarb. (*JAL* 335–36)

(Mrs. West is the conservative novelist Jane West whose 1796 novel *A Gossip's Story* probably influenced *Sense and Sensibility*.)

And yet there were always tradeoffs. To Anna, who is hoping that her aunt will visit her in Hendon during her stay in London at her brother Henry's establishment, Austen writes: "you mu[st be] aware that in another person's house one cannot command one's own time or activities, & though your Uncle Henry is so kind as to give us the use of a Carriage while we are with him, it may not be possible for us to turn that Carriage towards Hendon without a[c]tually mounting the Box ourselves" (*JAL* 295). Thus, too, the thoughtfulness of Henry Crawford's offering to come and take Fanny back from Portsmouth to Mansfield at the slightest hint delivered via his sister (*MP* III.11, 476) – and it's not just the oppressed dependent Fanny who is trapped in a place she would prefer to leave. Austen's more materially fortunate female protagonists experience quite similar restrictions on geographical movement. Mary Crawford benefits from having a brother at her disposal, and enough income between the two of them to afford the common luxuries of travel, but in reality it must have been a very small proportion of women indeed who had this kind of mobility.

It is a refrain throughout the novels, this thinking about women's dependence, the ways they were trapped as daughters and as wives. Maria Bertram is not an attractive character, but the novel shows her plight with a good deal of implicit empathy when we see her in the shrubbery uttering the famous words from Laurence Sterne's *Sentimental Journey* (1768): "I cannot get out, as the starling said" (*MP* I.10, 116). The education that Emma receives over the course of the novel that bears her name works partly to open her to greater insight and empathy: "The contrast between Mrs. Churchill's importance in the world, and Jane Fairfax's, struck her," the narrator tells us late in the book; "one was every thing, the other nothing—and she sat musing on the difference of woman's destiny" (E III.8, 417). So that though sociopolitical questions come in only very obliquely, creating an appearance of quietism that causes some readers to think irritably of Austen as a sort of village novelist for ladies, there is a good deal of evidence to counter that representation.

Austen's decision not to write explicitly about politics, in other words, must have been a deliberate choice rather than a matter of incapacity or lack of interest. Austen's niece Caroline, writing decades later, recounts this revealing anecdote:

> A very warm admirer of my Aunt's writing but a stranger in England, lately made the observation that it would be most interesting to know what had been Miss Austen's opinions on the great public events of her time—a period as she rightly observed, of the greatest interest—for my Aunt must have been a young woman, able to *think*, at the time of the French Revolution & the long disasterous chapter then begun, was closed by the battle of Waterloo, two years before her death—anyone *might* naturally desire to know what part such a mind as her's had taken in the great strifes of war and policy which so disquieted Europe for more than 20 years—and yet, it was a question that had never before presented itself to me—and tho' I have *now* retraced my steps on *this* track, I have found absolutely nothing!— (*MJA* 173)

She goes on to say that the family were strongly Tory, but that she can only guess what her aunt's orientation would have been to public events. We, too, are left guessing; it is only the politics of the family, not the politics of the nation, that Austen's fiction renders visible.

If domestic life as Austen presents it includes as many pains as pleasures, how does it come about that her fiction should be so widely thought of as inviting readers to escape into a world that lacks the unpleasantness and hard edges of daily reality? If you've read this book at all attentively, you will understand why I bristle at the notion that Austen wrote escapist fluff. These are serious books about people with real problems, even if they take place in drawing rooms rather than prisons or battlefields or factories or any of the other places, most of them associated more strongly with men's lives than with women's, that might be considered the domain of serious literature (a short-sighted view, something that Austen's fiction demonstrates by negative example).

The seeming avoidance of politics may be one of the factors that has made Austen's fiction – or, rather, the world her novels bring to life – such a powerful place of escape from our own lives and daily concerns. The fantasy of finding a refuge from economic and personal insecurity in a happy marriage is very strong in all of her novels, and the dream comes with an alluring collection of accessories (gowns, bonnets, ballrooms, carriages). Many of the works that have been produced under the sign of Austen (I am thinking especially of Georgette Heyer's novels and the whole genre of Regency romance fostered in the wake of their success) do indeed provide stories of wish-fulfilment par excellence, and the mode of light romantic comedy directly develops one aspect of Austen's storytelling.

While Austen's novels are frequently delightful to read, for reasons that include their verbal wit, broad situational comedy and gripping story-telling, they also explore the same questions about morality and community – what we owe to others and to ourselves – that concern the disciplines of political theory, sociology and psychology. They are hardly "escapist" in the sense that we usually use that word. And yet perhaps the idea that Austen's fiction needs defending along these lines is itself fundamentally misguided. It is an important quality of all great fiction that it is immersive; when I read a novel by Tolstoy or Dostoevsky or Flaubert or Woolf, I escape into the world of the novel, whether or not it has a happy ending, so that in some sense every novel is functionally escapist. Escapism is in that sense value-neutral – we escape into tragedy as well as comedy – and the quality of the escape has less to do with the nature of the outcome, positive or negative, than with the sheer immersive effect of the book's storytelling. On this count, Austen is surely one of the most powerful novelists who ever wrote. Her characters, as the Austen-besotted soldiers in Rudyard Kipling's 1926 story "The Janeites" like to attest, remain vividly alive to us even after we close the books' covers; alive, too, is Austen's vision of civility triumphant, manners and morals intertwined as a bulwark against violence and crudity, our own as well as that of other people and of the world at large.

Notes

Preface

1. On Austen and author-love, see especially the essays in *Janeites: Austen's Disciples and Devotees*, ed. Deidre Lynch (Princeton, NJ: Princeton University Press, 2000); and Claudia L. Johnson, "Austen Cults and Cultures," in *The Cambridge Companion to Jane Austen*, ed. Edward Copeland and Juliet McMaster, 2nd edn. (Cambridge: Cambridge University Press, 2010), 232–47. On the phenomenon of author-love more generally, see Helen Deutsch, *Loving Dr. Johnson* (Chicago: University of Chicago Press, 2005).
2. For further reading on this question, see Lisa Zunshine, *Why We Read Fiction: Theory of Mind and the Novel* (Columbus: Ohio State University Press, 2006); and Blakey Vermeule, *Why Do We Care about Literary Characters?* (Baltimore: Johns Hopkins University Press, 2010).
3. If you are inspired by Austen to turn to the discipline of sociology, you might enjoy Erving Goffman, *The Presentation of Self in Everyday Life* (New York: Doubleday, 1959); to ethics, Alasdair MacIntyre, *After Virtue: A Study in Moral Theory*, 2nd edn. (Notre Dame: University of Notre Dame Press, 1984).
4. A good recent account of the growth of Austen's reputation over the nineteenth century and beyond can be found in Devoney Looser, *The Making of Jane Austen* (Baltimore: Johns Hopkins University Press, 2017).

1 Letters

1. Susan E. Whyman, *The Pen and the People: English Letter Writers 1660–1800* (Oxford: Oxford University Press, 2009), 13.
2. "Jane Austen's Writing: A Technical Perspective," at www.themorgan.org/print/119.
3. Samuel Richardson, *Clarissa, or The History of a Young Lady* (1747–48), ed. Angus Ross (London: Penguin, 1985), L3, 47.
4. Tom Keymer, *Richardson's Clarissa and the Eighteenth-Century Reader* (Cambridge: Cambridge University Press, 1992), especially 1–32.

5. Choderlos de Laclos, *Dangerous Liaisons* (1782), trans. Helen Constantine (London: Penguin, 2007), 103.
6. James Raven, "Historical Introduction: The Novel Comes of Age," in James Raven and Antonia Forster, eds., with Stephen Bending, *The English Novel 1770–1829: A Bibliographical Survey of Prose Fiction Published in the British Isles, Vol. I: 1770–1799* (Oxford and New York: Oxford University Press, 2000), 15–121; the discussion is on 31, and a full table of epistolary titles as a proportion of total novels published per year during the period from 1770 to 1799 can be found on the following page.

2 Conversation

1. Claire Tomalin, *Jane Austen: A Life* (1997; New York: Random House, 1999), 68. Subsequent references to Tomalin's biography are to the American paperback edition and will be given parenthetically in the text.
2. For further discussion of the use during this period of inverted commas, previously a mark for annotation, in order to indicate both direct and indirect speech, see M. B. Parkes, *Pause and Effect: An Introduction to the History of Punctuation in the West* (Surrey: Ashgate, 1992), 93–94. I will also take this opportunity to thank my former doctoral student Katie Gemmill, who has taught me a great deal about the representation of conversation in eighteenth-century writing by way of her dissertation *Novel Conversations* (Columbia, PhD dissertation, 2016).

3 Revision

1. Carey McIntosh, *The Evolution of English Prose, 1700–1800: Style, Politeness, and Print Culture* (Cambridge: Cambridge University Press, 1998), 209–10.
2. See James McLaverty, *Pope, Print and Meaning* (Oxford: Oxford University Press, 2001), 2.
3. Jane Austen, *The History of England* (London: The British Library, 1993).
4. They are included as an appendix to the relevant volume of the Cambridge edition, whose editor, Peter Sabor, has also published several very interesting essays on Austen's *History of England*: Peter Sabor, "Jane Austen: Satirical Historian," in *Swift's Travels: Eighteenth-Century British Satire and Its Legacy*, ed. Nicholas Hudson and Aaron Santesso (Cambridge: Cambridge University Press, 2008), 217–32; and "Refashioning *The History of England*: Jane Austen and *1066 and All That*," in *The Afterlives of Eighteenth-Century Fiction*, ed. Daniel Cook and Nicholas Seager (Cambridge: Cambridge University Press, 2015), 273–89.

5. For a fuller discussion of this topic, see Douglas Lane Patey, *Probability and Literary Form: Philosophic Theory and Literary Practice in the Augustan Age* (Cambridge: Cambridge University Press, 1984), especially 197–98 and 218–19.

6. Roland Barthes, "The Reality Effect" (originally published in French in 1968), in *The Rustle of Language*, trans. Richard Howard (Berkeley and Los Angeles: University of California Press, 1989), 141–54.

7. Jan Marsh, *Christina Rossetti: A Literary Biography* (London: Jonathan Cape, 1994), 84.

8. Claudia L. Johnson, *Jane Austen: Women, Politics and the Novel* (Chicago and London: University of Chicago Press, 1988), 47–48.

9. This kind of narrative anomaly is rare in Austen, where we most often follow the perspective of a single character, but another interesting example can be found in *Sense and Sensibility*, volume III, chapter 3.

4 Manners

1. Bernard Mandeville, *The Fable of the Bees: or, Private Vices, Publick Benefits*, ed. F. B. Kaye, vol. 1 (Oxford: Clarendon, 1934; rpt. Indianapolis, IN: Liberty Fund, 1988), 53–54.

2. Albert O. Hirschman, *The Passions and the Interests: Political Arguments for Capitalism Before Its Triumph* (1977; Princeton, NJ: Princeton University Press, 2013).

3. For a very full account of Austen as what he calls "a theoretician of strategic thinking," see Michael Suk-Young Chwe, *Jane Austen: Game Theorist* (Princeton, NJ, and Oxford: Princeton University Press, 2013).

4. Austen seems to have taken the title "pride and prejudice" from a phrase that appears several times late in Burney's novel *Cecilia*, which depicts an aristocratic older female relative with considerably more sympathy; Austen's is a much harsher and more exaggerated caricature of a similar configuration of sociopolitical and cultural positionings. Frances Burney, *Cecilia, or Memoirs of an Heiress* (1782), ed. Peter Sabor and Margaret Anne Doody (Oxford and New York: Oxford University Press, 1988), V.x, 930–31.

5. Pierre Bourdieu, *Distinction: A Social Critique of the Judgement of Taste* (1979), trans. Richard Nice (Cambridge, MA: Harvard University Press, 1984), 6.

5 Morals

1. For a good discussion of this historical and intellectual context, see Hannah Arendt, *On Revolution*, intro. Jonathan Schell (1963; New York: Penguin, 2006), 86–89. William Godwin was pretty certainly England's most notorious proponent of absolute sincerity; for more detailed treatment of his

writings on truth and lying, see Jenny Davidson, *Hypocrisy and the Politics of Politeness: Manners and Morals from Locke to Austen* (Cambridge: Cambridge University Press, 2004), 91–95.

2. Edward W. Said, *Culture and Imperialism* (New York: Knopf, 1993), 96.

3. The classic and highly influential discussion of this topic is Lionel Trilling, "The Sentiment of Being and the Sentiments of Art," in *Sincerity and Authenticity* (Cambridge, MA: Harvard University Press, 1972), 53–80.

6 Voice

1. James Wood, *How Fiction Works* (New York: Farrar, Straus and Giroux/Picador, 2008), 19.

2. Dorrit Cohn, *Transparent Minds: Narrative Modes for Presenting Consciousness in Fiction* (Princeton, NJ: Princeton University Press, 1978), 112–13. Narrative theorist Mieke Bal provides a more detailed and extensive description of the workings of free indirect speech in *Narratology: Introduction to the Theory of Narrative*, 2nd edn. (1985; Toronto: University of Toronto Press, 1997), 46–52; and see also Ann Banfield, *Unspeakable Sentences: Narration and Representation in the Language of Fiction* (Boston and London: Routledge & Kegan Paul, 1982), esp. 228–35.

3. Claude Rawson, "Satire, Sensibility and Innovation in Jane Austen: *Persuasion* and the Minor Works," in *Satire and Sentiment, 1660–1830: Stress Points in the Augustan Tradition* (New Haven, CT, and London: Yale University Press, 1994), 267–98 (the citation is on 269).

4. Henry Fielding, *The History of Tom Jones, a Foundling*, ed. Alice Wakely and Thomas Keymer (London: Penguin, 2005), I.ii, 39.

5. Wayne Booth, *The Rhetoric of Fiction* (Chicago: University of Chicago Press, 1961), 216.

6. D. A. Miller, *Jane Austen, or The Secret of Style* (Princeton, NJ: Princeton University Press, 2003), 40–41.

7. For a fuller discussion of these passages, see Jenny Davidson, "Jane Austen and the Conditions of Knowledge," in *A Companion to British Literature: Volume III: Long Eighteenth-Century Literature 1660–1837*, ed. Robert DeMaria, Jr., Heesok Chang and Samantha Zucker (Chichester: John Wiley & Sons, Ltd., 2014), 298–311.

7 Female Economies

1. Tobias Smollett, *The Expedition of Humphry Clinker* (1771), ed. Evan Gottlieb, 2nd edn. (New York and London: W. W. Norton & Co., 2015), 129–31.

2. George Eliot, *Middlemarch*, ed. Bert G. Hornback, 2nd edn. (New York and London: W.W. Norton & Co., 2000), "Prelude," 3.

3. Andrew Miller, "Lives Unled in Realist Fiction," *Representations* 98 (Spring 2008): 118–34; the quotation is on 122.

4. Elizabeth Jane Howard, *The Light Years* (London: Macmillan, 1990), 201–02.

5. Ruth Perry, *Novel Relations: The Transformation of Kinship in English Literature and Culture, 1748–1818* (Cambridge: Cambridge University Press, 2004), 2–3, 38–42.

Guide to Further Reading

Eighteenth-Century Novels Mentioned in the Text

Frances Burney, *Cecilia, or Memoirs of an Heiress* (1782), ed. Peter Sabor and
  Margaret Anne Doody (Oxford and New York: Oxford University Press,
  1988).
Henry Fielding, *The History of Tom Jones, a Foundling* (1749), ed. Alice Wakely
  and Thomas Keymer (London: Penguin, 2005).
Johann Wolfgang von Goethe, *The Sorrows of Young Werther* (1774), trans.
  Burton Pike (New York: Modern Library, 2004).
Choderlos de Laclos, *Dangerous Liaisons* (1782), trans. Helen Constantine
  (London: Penguin, 2007).
Samuel Richardson, *Clarissa, or The History of a Young Lady* (1747–48), ed.
  Angus Ross (London: Penguin, 1985).
  Pamela, or, Virtue Rewarded (1740), ed. Thomas Keymer and Alice Wakely
  (Oxford and New York: Oxford University Press, 2001).
Tobias Smollett, *The Expedition of Humphry Clinker* (1771), ed. Evan Gottlieb,
  2nd cdn. (New York and London: W. W. Norton & Co., 2015), 129–31.
Laurence Sterne, *A Sentimental Journey and Other Writings*, ed. Tim Parnell and
  Ian Jack (Oxford: Oxford University Press, 2008).

Novels by Some of Austen's Female Contemporaries

Broadview Press has published accessible editions of many novels previously
  difficult to find in modern editions, and checking their chronological list of
  editions under the heading "Romantic Literature" will provide a much fuller
  selection.

Maria Edgeworth, *Belinda* (1801), ed. Kathryn J. Kirkpatrick (Oxford and
  New York: Oxford University Press, 1994).
  Patronage (1814), ed. Conor Carville, vols. 6–7 of *The Novels and Selected Works of
  Maria Edgeworth* (London and Brookfield, VT: Pickering & Chatto, 1999).

Susan Ferrier, *Marriage* (1818) (New York: Penguin; London: Virago, 1986).

Elizabeth Hamilton, *Memoirs of Modern Philosophers* (1800), ed. Claire Grogan (Peterborough, ON: Broadview, 2000).

Elizabeth Inchbald, *A Simple Story* (1791), ed. Anna Lott (Peterborough, ON: Broadview, 2006).

Amelia Opie, *Adeline Mowbray, or, The Mother and Daughter* (1804), ed. Anne McWhir (Peterborough, ON: Broadview, 2010).

Mary Wollstonecraft, *Mary, a Fiction and The Wrongs of Woman, or, Maria* (1788, 1798), ed. Michelle Faubert (Peterborough, ON: Broadview, 2012).

Contexts on Gender and Politics

Marilyn Butler, *Burke, Paine, Godwin, and the Revolution Controversy* (Cambridge and New York: Cambridge University Press, 1984).

Linda Colley, *Britons: Forging the Nation, 1707–1837* (New Haven, CT: Yale University Press, 1992).

Claudia L. Johnson, *Equivocal Beings: Politics, Gender, and Sentimentality in the 1790s: Wollstonecraft, Radcliffe, Burney, Austen* (Chicago: University of Chicago Press, 1995).

Claire Tomalin, *Jane Austen: A Life* (1997; New York: Random House, 1999).

Mary Wollstonecraft, *A Vindication of the Rights of Woman* (1792), ed. Deidre Shauna Lynch (New York: W. W. Norton, 2009).

Austen's Reception and Posthumous Reputation

Claudia L. Johnson, "Austen Cults and Cultures," in *The Cambridge Companion to Jane Austen*, 2nd edn., ed. Edward Copeland and Juliet McMaster (Cambridge: Cambridge University Press, 2010).

Devoney Looser, *The Making of Jane Austen* (Baltimore: Johns Hopkins University Press, 2017).

Deidre Lynch, ed. *Janeites: Austen's Disciples and Devotees* (Princeton, NJ: Princeton University Press, 2000).

Austen Criticism

Marilyn Butler, *Jane Austen and the War of Ideas* (Oxford: Clarendon, 1975).

Michael Suk-Young Chwe, *Jane Austen: Game Theorist* (Princeton, NJ, and Oxford: Princeton University Press, 2013).

Jenny Davidson, *Hypocrisy and the Politics of Politeness: Manners and Morals from Locke to Austen* (Cambridge: Cambridge University Press, 2004).

"Jane Austen and the Conditions of Knowledge," in *A Companion to British Literature: Volume III: Long Eighteenth-Century Literature 1660–1837*, ed. Robert DeMaria Jr., Heesok Chang and Samantha Zucker (Chichester: John Wiley & Sons, Ltd., 2014), 298–311.

Claudia L. Johnson, *Jane Austen: Women, Politics and the Novel* (Chicago and London: University of Chicago Press, 1988).

D. A. Miller, *Jane Austen, or The Secret of Style* (Princeton, NJ: Princeton University Press, 2003), 40–41.

Claude Rawson, "Satire, Sensibility and Innovation in Jane Austen: *Persuasion* and the Minor Works," in *Satire and Sentiment, 1660–1830: Stress Points in the Augustan Tradition* (New Haven, CT, and London: Yale University Press, 1994), 267–98.

Peter Sabor, "Jane Austen: Satirical Historian," in *Swift's Travels: Eighteenth-Century British Satire and Its Legacy*, ed. Nicholas Hudson and Aaron Santesso (Cambridge: Cambridge University Press, 2008), 217–32.

"Refashioning *The History of England*: Jane Austen and *1066 and All That*," in *The Afterlives of Eighteenth-Century Fiction*, ed. Daniel Cook and Nicholas Seager (Cambridge: Cambridge University Press, 2015), 273–89.

Edward W. Said, *Culture and Imperialism* (New York: Knopf, 1993).

Patricia Meyer Spacks, *Gossip* (New York: Knopf, 1985).

Tony Tanner, *Jane Austen* (Basingstoke: Macmillan, 1986).

Lionel Trilling, "The Sentiment of Being and the Sentiments of Art," in *Sincerity and Authenticity* (Cambridge, MA: Harvard University Press, 1972), 53–80.

Literary Criticism on Related Topics

Helen Deutsch, *Loving Dr. Johnson* (Chicago: University of Chicago Press, 2005).

Tom Keymer, *Richardson's Clarissa and the Eighteenth-Century Reader* (Cambridge: Cambridge University Press, 1992).

Andrew Miller, "Lives Unled in Realist Fiction," *Representations* 98 (Spring 2008): 118–34.

Douglas Lane Patey, *Probability and Literary Form: Philosophic Theory and Literary Practice in the Augustan Age* (Cambridge: Cambridge University Press, 1984).

Ruth Perry, *Novel Relations: The Transformation of Kinship in English Literature and Culture, 1748–1818* (Cambridge: Cambridge University Press, 2004).

Blakey Vermeule, *Why Do We Care about Literary Characters?* (Baltimore: Johns Hopkins University Press, 2010).

Lisa Zunshine, *Why We Read Fiction: Theory of Mind and the Novel* (Columbus: Ohio State University Press, 2006).

Novels and Narration

Mieke Bal, *Narratology: Introduction to the Theory of Narrative*, 2nd edn. (1985; Toronto: University of Toronto Press, 1997).

Ann Banfield, *Unspeakable Sentences: Narration and Representation in the Language of Fiction* (Boston and London: Routledge & Kegan Paul, 1982).

Roland Barthes, "The Reality Effect" (originally published in French in 1968), in *The Rustle of Language*, trans. Richard Howard (Berkeley and Los Angeles: University of California Press, 1989), 141–54.

Wayne Booth, *The Rhetoric of Fiction* (Chicago: University of Chicago Press, 1961), 216.

Dorrit Cohn, *Transparent Minds: Narrative Modes for Presenting Consciousness in Fiction* (Princeton, NJ: Princeton University Press, 1978).

James Wood, *How Fiction Works* (New York: Farrar, Straus and Giroux/Picador, 2008).

Austen and the Social Sciences

Only a few of these books mention Austen specifically, but each offers something of value in illuminating Austen's treatment of human values and behavior.

Hannah Arendt, *On Revolution*, intro. Jonathan Schell (1963; New York: Penguin, 2006).

Pierre Bourdieu, *Distinction: A Social Critique of the Judgement of Taste* (1979), trans. Richard Nice (Cambridge, MA: Harvard University Press, 1984).

Erving Goffman, *The Presentation of Self in Everyday Life* (New York: Doubleday, 1959).

Albert O. Hirschman, *The Passions and the Interests: Political Arguments for Capitalism Before Its Triumph* (1977; Princeton, NJ: Princeton University Press, 2013).

Alasdair MacIntyre, *After Virtue: A Study in Moral Theory*, 2nd edn. (Notre Dame, IN: University of Notre Dame Press, 1984).

Judith Shklar, *Ordinary Vices* (Cambridge, MA: Belknap Press of Harvard University Press, 1984).

Index

Printed in the United States
By Bookmasters